Merry Christmas
2017
With our love
B ÷ B

Lanterns of the Soul

A Poetic Journey through Life

Lanterns
of the Soul

A Poetic Journey through Life

Lynda Harris

iUniverse, Inc.
Bloomington

Lanterns of the Soul
A Poetic Journey through Life

iUniverse books may be ordered through booksellers or by contacting:

iUniverse
1663 Liberty Drive
Bloomington, IN 47403
www.iuniverse.com
1-800-Authors (1-800-288-4677)

ISBN: 978-1-4502-7623-8 (sc)
ISBN: 978-1-4502-7625-2 (hc)
ISBN: 978-1-4502-7624-5 (ebk)

Library of Congress Control Number: 2011902749

Printed in the United States of America

iUniverse rev. date: 03/23/2011

Dedicated to Harold Willson.

Harold Willson was my uncle. He died of polio when only in his early twenties. My mother has told me that he loved to write poetry and that my own passion for it was definitely handed down to me from him. Because of his shortened life, he was unable to pursue his hobby as I have been allowed to do.

This is for him.

A Letter Just the Same

I'm writing to you, Uncle Harold,
Though you're one I never knew,
To tell you that your love of poems
Was passed to me from you.

I'm well aware you know me not,
For I was very young
That day the angels called your name
And beckoned you to come.

Your sister Mary's oldest girl—
They often call me Lynn—
For it is I who writes these words—
All grown, the child you knew back then.

Perhaps there'll be a day in time—
When I meet eternity—
That you and I can sit and share
This love we have of poetry.

I wonder if it thrilled you so
The way it does for me
To phrase your thoughts in rhythmic form
And have them rhyme in harmony.

And did you ever feel the joy,
When finally you were through,
To read the poem you'd written,
To know it belonged to you?

I'm sure you felt this love of yours
Did surely come from God.
So, did you feel, at writing's end,
Him give your poem a nod?

I, too, have felt it many times,
This approval from Above,
As if I'm giving back to Him
What He endowed to me with love.

I wish I could have known you well.
What fun it would have been
Exchanging back and forth our poems,
Becoming quite good friends.

But it was simply not to be
The joy that could have been;
But even so, I'm signing this
To Uncle Harold, Love from Lynn.

~

October 1985

And also to my three beautiful daughters,
Anna, Melanie, and Meghan …

Without whom this book would simply not have
been possible. They have inspired me, encouraged me,
devoted so much of their time, and stood by me every
step of the way.

This book belongs to them too.

~

Contents

I

Introduction

So many times in my life as I have lived and experienced each mothering moment, witnessed all of the wonderment and awe that only God could create, and pondered each day filled with love and questions, I have so often felt the words of a poem forming in my mind. In search of the right words to express my thoughts and emotions, I would pick up my pen and turn on my lantern - the one that shines directly into my soul.

My poems are my own poetic journey through life. Having started composing in my early teens and continuing to where I am in my life today, my book *of Lanterns* reflects my journey beginning with my earliest to my most recent.

Good Day To You

It's only me, my pad and pen,
My thoughts while drifting by.
A very private love affair,
This poetry and I.
Whoever may be reading this,
I hope you're well today
And void of any heartache,
So joy can come your way.
And also, I am hoping
That maybe you have known
Some simple little pleasure
Like these poems I call my own.

~

II

A Lantern on Love and Family

My Home

All my life there's always been
A place I've called my own.
Not just walls that dwell within
But something I call *home*.

Unlike paint that soon will fade,
But with security and trust,
These walls have all been firmly made
With tools that will not rust.

I pass each day in a set routine
Like I passed the one before,
But I count the hours in between
Till I walk back through my own front door.

When I'm at home, I don't compete
With my fellow peers.
I do not feel I've met defeat,
As I do when they are near.

At home, I like to turn the key
And lock the world outside.
I often wish they'd not include me
On their passing rides.

All my life, I plan to save
This warmth I've had at home.
And maybe someday I can say
I passed it on to walls *I own*.

~

Early 1960s

At Carnival Time

The children are happy; their faces are bright;
They laugh and yell in all their delight.
Some young, some old, some big, some small
Have gathered here, oh one and all
　　　At Carnival Time

In the middle of the night, the spotlights glare
Upon the activities of the fair.
There's much to be seen; there's much to be heard.
It doesn't take much for the crowd to get stirred
　　　At Carnival Time

Love also lingers in the air
For that loving couple whose lips will share
The secret of a kiss revealed
While high in the air on a Ferris wheel
　　　At Carnival Time

~

Early 1960s

Last Night I Flew

I flew through the trees
I flew through the air
I flew on a breeze—
But I didn't care!

I flew through the sky
Over land, over sea
I flew oh so high—
Just look at me!

I flew through a cloud
So fleecy and white
To the angels I bowed—
While flying at night!

I flew above trains
I flew above cars.
I felt like a plane—
Heading for Mars!

I flew above people
I flew above towns
I just missed a steeple—
But I won't come down!

Gee, what fun
To fly like a bird
To talk to the sun—
Yet never be heard!

To wink at the stars
Or play with the rain
To fly away far—
And come back again!

But as the day breaks
My flying soon ends.
I will have to wake—
A new day begins!

~

Early 1960s

Halloween Night

Halloween night is a spooky one—
The night when witches and ghosts all come.
The moon shines bright across the sky
As all the bats go flying by.

The kids are yelling "Trick or treat!"
With floppy hats and tails on seats.
Soon a bang is at the door—
Another gang is back for more.

They all want candy, lots to eat—
For after all, it's trick or treat.
Different costumes all disguise
Beneath them little glowing eyes.

Witches, ghosts, cats, and brooms,
Gobblers, pumpkins, and the moon.
Each takes a bow in all delight
As they are part of Halloween Night.

~

October 1963

The Bathroom Massacre

This morning—10:00 AM—
The famous massacre began.
The killer, anxious for his prey,
Found it on the bathroom tray.

The victim—too tiny to fight—
Squirmed around in fright.
Shaking with all his might,
He sat there, turning white.

The killer—not as little—
Grabbed the victim round his middle.
He squeezed and squeezed the little guy,
The victim oozing out his cry.

The killer went back for more.
The victim's middle now quite sore.
Still, with stuff gushing forth,
The little guy could stand no more.

The killer left—smiling—
The victim was dying.
The killer would no doubt return—
Of that, the little guy felt sure…

The time—12:00 AM—
The massacre begins again.
The little guy is squeezed once more—
Around his middle as before …

How can we prevent
Crimes like these events?
Well, the moral's this:
Do not abuse …
Your old, your loyal toothpaste tube!

~

Early 1960s

Hush, Don't You Cry

Hush, Don't You Cry

This is a ballad telling the story of a poor, young pioneer woman, who, after being married for only two years, lost her husband to another woman. Sitting outside on her porch one evening watching the sun go down, she reminisces while rocking her baby to sleep …

Down in the valley,
The valley so blue,
I lost my poor darling,
I lost him to her.

He gave me two years,
Two years filled with love.
But I've lost my sweet man,
Love wasn't enough.

He built me a home,
And I gave him a child.
But now I'm alone,
Alone all the while.

Down in the valley,
This valley so blue,
He used to love me
But now he loves you.

I'm sittin' here rockin'
His child on my knee.
I'm sittin' here thinkin'
How his pa once loved me.

The sun is a'lowerin'
Behind the tall slopes.
My baby's a'sleepin'
And I'm cryin' for hope.

I loved my sweet man,
And he loved me too.
Till she came along
To our valley so blue.

I beg of you, Lord,
To send us someone.
A new man for myself,
A new pa for my son.

Let him be good
And lead a straight path.
Have him to love us
As no man yet has.

I gaze at this child,
Asleep in my arms.
And my lips form a smile
At this bundle of charm.

So my sweetheart is gone
To return no more.
But he did leave behind
This child I adore.

As I start to arise
I look to the slopes,
And a voice seems to say,
"Your child is your hope."

My baby's a'weepin',
Now, hush, don't you cry.
I'll sing you a song
Of days gone by …

Down in the valley
The valley so blue.
I lost my poor darling—
I lost him to her.

~

Mid 1960s

My Father's Love

Tonight I felt so all alone—
I soon began to weep.
I've not a love to call my own
Yet so much love to keep.

Beside my bed, with no one near,
I sat and cried some more.
Until at last despite my tears,
I saw a man walk through my door.

He came and sat upon my bed.
He kissed and stroked my hair.
Although a word was never said,
I knew, at least, he cared.

It seemed as if he understood
This longing in my heart.
His arms about me felt so good—
My tears grew far apart.

This man means *oh* so much to me
And to the One above—
With all my heart, I pray to Thee
To thank you for, my father's love.

~

Late 1960s

Why Can't I Too Know Love?

I just don't understand
Whatever is His plan.
I only ask of You above
Why can't I too know love?

I'm young and yet can feel
I want a love that's real.
Not one that's flighty, wild, and free
But one to love a girl like me.

I'd only wish for simple joys—
Like holding hands with this one boy.
I'd share his laugh; I'd share his tears.
If just to have him always near.

Why keep this boy and me apart
When all this love is in my heart?
I only ask of You, above,
Why can't I too know love?

~

Mid 1960s

Shy Love

If I had but just one dream
I'm sure of what it'd be—
To meet the boy who really seems
To mean the world to me.

He is not all that I'd prefer
In looking for a man.
But no boy's perfect, I am sure,
So get the next best if you can.

When 'ere he looks at me and smiles,
I want to breathe a sigh.
At him, I'd like to stare awhile—
Instead, I just say, hi.

I'd like to think he feels the same,
But how am I to know?
He might not even know my name,
But I know his, and more.

~

Late 1960s

The Special One

I met a boy some months ago—
He looked at me and said hello.
I replied and sent a smile,
And that was all for a little while.

Soon we found ourselves a'talking
On the way to class as we went walking.
Now we are the best of friends—
I hope that it will never end.

He's tall and handsome, hair of brown,
Always a grin and never a frown.
Kind and gentle he seems to be,
Respectful and courteous when he's with me.

I wish I knew what's on his mind—
Does he look at me and try to find
A way to tell me that he cares
And wants our friendship to be shared?

If only he would think to say
Something nice in a special way.
Perhaps he'll come to realize
Just what are in my hopeful eyes.

~

Late 1960s

Long, Lonely Night

He comes on over every night,
Which seems to make my day end right.
He's at my side, and all the while
Offering through the night, his smiles.
His hand is there for me to hold.
He whispers things I like to know.
We laugh and talk and watch TV
Until the time he turns to me
And says it's late, that he must go ...
So I sadly watch him leave my door.
But as I turn to go upstairs,
A deep contentment fills the air—
Because my love was here with me,
The night was short but very sweet.

Tonight was very different though—
He couldn't come; I missed him so.
I missed his touch and warm embrace;
I missed the smile upon his face.
I missed the hands I like to hold,
The things I'm used to being told.
I missed the arms that 'round me go;
I missed the way he holds me so.
There wasn't much to fill the time
That suddenly was only mine.
At last, when I did go upstairs
I missed the sweetness in the air.
But across my room to switch the light,
I smiled good-bye, long, lonely night.

~

August 1970—to Carroll Matthew Harris, with all my love.

Make Him See

Oh Lord, see fit to make him see
The time has come to marry me.
I can't go on … I must go on—
My love for him is just too strong.

"This girl beside me, I thee wed …"
The tune keeps running through my head.
My thoughts keep turning to the time
He'll gaze at me and say those lines.

Surely he can see the way
We love each other more each day.
I do so want and badly need him—
Oh Lord, give strength to keep from sin.

For thirteen months, it seems somehow
We've both already said those vows …
Unspoken words—it would not hurt
To say them aloud within a church.

For better or worse … Oh let him sing
While slipping on the tiny ring.
Make us one and let my life
Continue on—but as his wife.

Make him see how good it'd be—
Our tiny home, just him and me.
Sharing, giving, making dreams,
Always doing as a team.

Help him come to understand
He needn't be rich to get my hand—
It will not hurt to just make do
With a little less for a year or two.

Make him want as much as I,
And help him see the reasons why
We can't continue on as two
But have to join and say, "I do."

Till death do part, oh, let it be;
Unite and make us one in Thee.
Oh God, don't make it long until
We kneel to Thee and say, "I will."

~

March 1971

To CM on Our First Wedding Anniversary
October 16, 1972

A card—a verse—some mushy lines
Don't turn you on, I know.
But maybe if the words are mine,
They'll mean a little more.

I don't intend to make this long—
Just only to reveal
The ever-present happy song
Of loving thoughts I feel.
Our wedding vows are one year old,
And each day I love you more.
But sweetheart, you can never know
The amount I have in store.

For deep within there's happiness,
A joy that fills my life.
'Cause sweetheart I feel truly blessed:
It's a privilege to be your wife.

~

Marriage at Three

It's late—the clock reads five to three,
The world's asleep; there's only me.
The stillness screams its presence known:
It knows I hate to be alone.

I fight to find a quiet place
To rest my thoughts and keep them safe.
Instead, the darkness circles round—
With every turn, it pins me down.

I squirm from somewhere deep within—
My being says it cannot win.
I turn in time! Now I smile:
Love was with me all the while.

I laugh; I sigh and whisper low
"Turn back darkness; turn and go.
You cannot hurt me—can't you see?
He's lying right here next to me."

His handsome form beside me lies.
His breathing sounds the gentle sighs
Of one who lays in perfect peace.
He doesn't know I watch him sleep.

Above a strong and towering chest;
His hands are folded as in rest.
His finger wears a shiny band—
Its mate is found on my left hand.

His tousled hair—no order now
Gently falls upon his brow.
Eyes that smile and tell a tale
Are sleeping now behind their veil.

He rests upon his favorite side,
But now his limbs are stretching wide …
He turns and stirs, but finally then
Returns to unknown depths again.

And then I start to cry within,
Please wait and let me follow him.
I snuggle close and whisper, "Please,
Let me venture down with thee."

He stirs, awakens, says hello—
Unaware of what I know.
His arm goes round and draws me near;
He doesn't know he's fought my fear.

I close my eyes and welcome sleep,
Until the dawn, the dark will keep.
I turn; I stir; and finally then,
I see the unknown depths again.

February 1973

Marital Communion

Our naked souls entwined as one,
Two beating hearts are we:
Most holy of all communions
Is the act of love in Thee.

Blessed in awareness, enabled to feel,
Permitted the pleasure of touch,
Privileged to answer the desperate appeals
Of the one we love so much.

This sacred way of love expressed—
The anticipation too—
Its joyous warmth could not be blessed
Unless approved by You.

A time to pause, an hour spent,
Renewed forgotten vows.
Repeating thoughts that came and went:
There's time to say them now.

And so bathed in contentment
Of our love reassured,
We are clothed in commitment
To each other's word.

Though bent in desire to continue forever
These moments so precious and few;
We know we cannot, and therefore endeavor
To gratefully return them to You.

~

March 1973

He Won't Pick Up My Hand

When we were young and skipping out
Going here and there about
My every wish was his demand—
But he never would pick up my hand.

He swept me off my feet back then,
And before too long, I married him.
And now he loves me all he can;
'Cept he hardly ever holds my hand.

He sees to all my wants and needs;
A home and child he's given me.
A strong and very abled man—
But he never thinks to hold my hand.

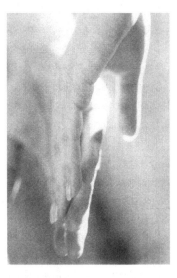

He'd risk his very life for me
And would do it very willingly.
So in a crowd, you'd think he'd stand
Close to me and take my hand.

It's just my love for him is such …
It warms me still to feel his touch.
I wish the thought would somehow scan
Across his mind to hold my hand.

And so I'll wait and cradle deep
This ever longing that I keep.
The warmth will come when 'ere he can
Let go himself and hold my hand.

~

January 1976

How Sad

How sad for a woman, a mother-to-be
If her husband shares not their expectancy.
How sad this miracle which comes from above
Is not enjoyed by the one she most loves.

When she quietly tells him the news she bears—
That she carries his baby and a child will be theirs—
How sad when her happiness sets like the sun
When she hears that he's asking, "What have you done?"

How sad that the planning and waiting ahead
Has to be done by her instead.
For she knows when they talk of their baby to come
That he finds it hard to share in the fun.

As her body matures and their baby grows,
She's very proud for all to know.
But, oh how sad, if the father-to-be
Prefers that others should not see.

When new life starts to stir within,
She quickly goes to share with him.
But when she does, his look reveals
It's something he simply cannot feel.

How sad when she knows he doesn't share
Her fun in buying the rocking chair.
The diapers, booties, or safety pins
Just don't seem to interest him.

How sad—she longs to hear him say
She's not to blame in any way ...
That now he feels and wants and sees
This little child of theirs to be.

How sad she cannot make him feel
How very beautiful and real
It is to carry deep within
So very much a part of him.

How sad that now her time is nigh,
While wheeled away, he's standing by.
He smiles, for now he knows he's glad…
She turns to see too late—how sad.

~

January 1974

To Grandmother and Granddaddy from One to Be

Although I'm very little now
I seem to know you both somehow.
Just you wait; before you know
I'll pop right out and say hello.

For someone quite as small as me
I really know a lot, you see.
I've looked around and I approve—
I'm gonna like my little move.

I know I'll love your friendly home:
There's lots of room for me to roam.
I'm sure the stairs are fun to climb—
But many falls I know are mine.

I'm sure my mom will gladly use
Your rocking chair until I snooze.
And when I blink and bob my head
She'll gently lay me on your bed.

I know the porch is sure to be
A favorite playground just for me.
I'll blow my whistle, toot my horn,
And not get wet if it should storm.

I know about my daddy's farm:
I've chased the cows and seen the barn.
The grassy meadow and mountain stream
Are spots where I've already been.

Before I even came to be
My mommy always thought of me.
Whenever Mommy goes somewhere
She likes to play that I am there.

And so I've seen an awful lot
For still so small a tiny tot.
I've been imagined everywhere—
How it will be when I am there.

How nice when we will finally be
Daddy, Mommy, little me.
I hope they'll let me stay with you
Now and then, a day or two.

I think that Daddy's gonna be
Pretty fairly strict with me.
And Mommy's gonna make me mind
Whenever I am out of line.

How nice when I am with you all
If I'm not made to stand as tall.
Maybe you will let me see
A little of the imp in me.

I think perhaps I'd better go—
I've got a long long way to grow.
How nice for me that I exist—
No more a dream or something wished.

Forgive me, if at first I'm shy—
I'm bound to be when I arrive.
But pretty soon, I'll come to know
To run and hug you both hello.

~

1974

Quiet Day
for Anna

As I rise to greet my baby's cries
With stumbling feet and weary eyes
I make my way unto her bed
Which all night held her sleeping head.

I marvel how she always knows
When dawn arrives and evening goes;
Like the bell that chimes the hour's near
She coos aloud that morning's here.

Her smile awakens, stirs my heart
And makes my sleepy thoughts depart.
I long to have her know the way
She brings a joy to every day.

I peer outside and view the rain
And think it must be cold again.
And so decide to stay at home—
We'll spend a quiet day alone.

I have no chores; my work is done
So I set aside this time for fun.
We play and bounce upon the floor
And she laughs the giggle I adore.

She's still quite small and tires soon
So I gently tote her to her room.
I enjoy the time to knit or read
While she sweetly takes the nap she needs.

In hardly any time at all
I hear a coo from down the hall.
Once again, our play resumes
And passes by the afternoon.

Evening shadows soon appear
To indicate that night is near.
I gently lay my daughter down
And try to kiss away her frown.

Tomorrow may not be as slow—
Most likely we'll be on the go.
But little sweetheart, let me say
I've so enjoyed our quiet day.

~

September 1975

I'm the Mother of a Two-Year-Old

There are times I think that I should wear
A sign that says APPROACH WITH CARE!
And clearly printed right below:
I'M THE MOTHER OF A TWO-YEAR-OLD!

I always used to be on time
And never carried but a dime.
But now I'm late for this and that
And toting dolls and training pants.

I didn't know, nor did I ask
About this monumental task.
The months of infancy were few
For now, my little girl is two.

Eternal time is thus her friend—
To her a minute never ends.
The time of day is no concern
To a little girl who's out to learn.

If allowed to have the upper hand
She'd never sit; she'd have to stand.
Nor would she eat or take a nap;
She hasn't time for things like that.

But let her have a dresser drawer
With which to empty on the floor
Or let her play with silks and lace
And then you'll see a happy face.

She wants to follow everywhere—
Down the hall or up the stairs.
In the bathroom, by the stove:
Always there, my two year old.

She wants to mimic all she sees
From washing clothes to raking leaves.
In the house or out of doors
She wants to help with all the chores.

She loves to use the telephone
And likes to hold it on her own.
She talks away and just pretends
There's someone on the other end.

Bless this child You gave to us
Who runs and romps from dawn to dusk.
Guard her well in every way
When fast asleep or hard at play.

Oh Lord, a nuisance she can be.
A bigger pest you'll never see.
She's starting now to sass us back
And teases with a certain laugh.

By end of day, I'm all worn out
While she's still frolicking about.
Her chitter-chatter knows no peace—
Her questions never seem to cease.

It's amazing, though, to watch her learn;
She grabs at life at every turn.
Her little pigtails can't keep time;
They seem to fly a step behind.

Dear me, this precious little girl
Blue-eyed and blonde with many curls.
Today angelic, tomorrow wild.
I love you so, my little child.

Come; sit upon my lap awhile,
We'll cuddle close and share a smile.
Let's linger long and hurry not—
Stay a minute more, sweetheart.

Be still for now and hesitate;
Your little life can surely wait.
For Mommy wants so much to hold
Her lovely, lively two-year-old.

~

1977

In Memoriam

> In loving memory of my grandmother, Edith Willson

At peace and rest, her journey made,
The seasons of her life are staid.
She lingers not; no never more,
But answered the call to Eternity's door.

Timelessness is hard to see:
To imagine it to even be.
But if forever exists somewhere
Then know for sure that she is there.

To say she's gone is too extreme,
For just because she lived, she's been.
Her person walked amidst us once,
And now her soul remains with us.

Her age'd years were well fought out
With memories many, to dwell about.
Her painful, happy times, now one,
Her storms are gone; there's just bright sun.

She left not wealth and neither fame,
A simple lady unacclaimed.
It matters not, for we, her seeds
Have known and loved this soul called Ede.

~

March 1976

One More Time

One More Time

I wrote this story in 1978 before I became pregnant with Melanie. It expresses the very deep desire I had within me to have another baby and to have Anna become a sister. Because of the title and basic theme, I often refer to Melanie as "my little once more."

One more time, I am going to allow myself to have a baby.

One more time, I am going to know that somewhere deep inside me there is a little something that someday will be as big and complete as Anna. One more time to know the incredibleness that, because of a simple positive test, someone really must be in there, even though I don't look any different.

One more time, I am going to feel a baby kick inside me—to know the excitement and the occasional pain of it.

One more time to wonder whether I am carrying a small baby boy or a small baby girl.

One more time—and this time to appreciate the entire process so much more, because of my experience with Anna.

One more time, I want to go to the hospital to give birth to a baby. My baby. One more time, I want to see my baby born. One more time to hear the doctor say, "See that, that is the hair on his head." To think, my God, that little bit of hair I see inside me is the hair on my little baby's head—the little baby who is still unborn and who I still don't know and have never seen. But he *is* in there, after all. I can finally see part of him!

One more time, I want to be shown a bundle in a blanket, with only the smallest little round face peeking through, fresh from my body—a total stranger and yet taken from me—and to know that someday I will know him or her like my right hand, as I do Anna. I want to enjoy my wisdom, given to me through my experience with Anna, to know and enjoy the split-second miracle that your baby is only a stranger to you once—at that very moment of first viewing. Forever after, he or she is yours, without any doubt, no more that tiny stranger. It is fascinating to be aware of, and well worth appreciating, this split-second miracle.

It's strange that I'm ready. Six months ago I wasn't. But now that Anna is three, I am where I wanted to be. My mind is prepared for it, and I'm ready to get my body prepared for it—one more time.

One more time, I want to do this—for Anna. I want to enjoy what must be a wonderful experience—Anna becoming a sister to someone. To watch her excitement as she feels the baby kick, to see her face the first time she sees the face of our new baby, to see her pure joy at being able to be so much help to me. To see her *be* a sister.

One more time, I want to subject myself to enduring the complete frustration that can ride over you like a tidal wave and leave you partially paralyzed with the insanity that comes with rearing a child. Children are frustrating, aggravating, annoying, disturbing, sleep-stealing, insanity-producing, noisy, interrupting, careless, clumsy, often stupid and fussy and irritable, forever whiny, and—above all— time consuming. I will not tell a lie.

There is one small catch: at the exact moment that they are being the above, they are secretly preparing themselves to turning right around in the *next moment* to being the very opposite and, thereby, erasing the negative act. It is terribly confusing to be a parent—how children can perform such a feat, and restore *part of* the sanity you thought for sure you had lost. On behalf of the child, I cannot tell a lie.

One more time, I want to give up a little bit more of the togetherness that my husband and I have left since having our first baby. But why, when children can be such a mess? Because marital togetherness is *not everything,* is *not all-important,* is *not the only thing*. There is something above and beyond. After three years with Anna, I have suddenly realized that and why.

One more time, I want to see that stranger in the bundle, who knows no one, and get to the time when I hear him or her say, "Mommy," and then to the time when I can ask, "*Who* is your Mommy?" and hear him or her proudly say, "Lynda is!" Anna finally understands that her mommy is a person, too, and has a name, and that is such a beautiful accomplishment for both Mother and daughter. I want that ... one more time.

One more time, I want to see my husband hold a baby and later walk behind a child, knowing that child is his and that it came from him.

So why is it worth it, to give up total togetherness between a husband and wife? Because when babies finally turn three years old, they finally see, hear, touch, smell, taste, think, question, understand, laugh, grieve, cry, reason, and do everything that we do. Anna does all these things now. She is a complete and total person. That total togetherness that my husband and I gave up *is* <u>Anna</u>. As she turns three, you can actually see that which we once gave up abstractly. You are given back that total togetherness that you thought you had lost. And it is even better than before. A complete child, *our c*hild. Someone we can watch and study and grow up with. We couldn't do that with what we had before. You cannot actually hold in your arms the oneness of a husband and wife. But after the birth of a child, you can love and hold close against you that which you gave up. It *is* worth it.

I want that … *one more time.*

~

Mid 1978

Melanie

How gently in her crib she sleeps,
How sweet her tiny hands and feet.
How soft her hair, a button nose,
Ten little fingers, ten little toes.

Though time may go, I'll not forget
The warmth I felt when first we met.
I held you close that early morn
Just minutes after you were born.

With you awake—and so alert—
I soon forgot the pain and hurt.
You stared at me; I stared at you,
And total joy was what I knew.

I used to say, "Just one more time
I'd like to bear a child of mine."
And so I did, and here you are:
Another girl to steal my heart.

A few short months and you have won
So much love from everyone.
You're such a quiet, little dear:
One hardly knows you're even here.

You have a lot to learn, it's true.
And so your sister waits for you,
To be your friend and lend a hand
And help you when she feels she can.

You can't remain this small, I know;
The hands of time will make you grow.
Until they do, sleep peacefully,
My precious, little Melanie.

~

August 1979

My Song to Anna Katherine
   (Sung to the tune of "Happy Birthday")

Anna Katherine are you
      A daughter and sister, too.
You're the one I always dreamed of,
      My little angel of love.

Momma loved you yesterday,
      Momma loves you today.
Momma loves you tomorrow,
      Momma loves you always.

You're the sweetest thing I've seen,
      You're the sweetest thing I know.
You're sweet as a dream,
      And I love you so.

I pray for you a long life,
      Full of happiness, no strife.
May all your dreams come true;
      May God be with you.

~

1980

My Song to Melanie Amanda
(Sung to the tune of "Happy Birthday")

Little Melanie are you;
    A daughter and sister, too,
I call you my "little once more";
    You're the child I adore.

Momma loved you yesterday,
    Momma loves you today.
Momma loves you tomorrow,
    Momma loves you always.

You're the sweetest thing I've seen,
    You're the sweetest thing I know,
You're sweet as a dream,
    And I love you so.

I pray for you a long life,
    Full of happiness, no strife.
May all your dreams come true;
    May God be with you.

~

1979

God Bless You

God bless you on your journey
Till you meet a certain day
When you sit upon your bed
And say, "I think I feel okay."

God bless you on your journey
Through your pain and sleepless nights,
While faithfully declaring
"I won't give up this fight."

God bless you on your journey
Through a mile of caring friends
Whose questions of "How are You?"
Never seem to end.

God bless you on your journey
As forever more you pray
Reaching out and upward
To Him who said today,

"I do grant you one more journey,
For your life is still so dear.
I find I'm not quite ready
To have you join Me Here."

God bless your onward living
(It seems to be His will).
May His peace surround you
And His grace go with you still.

~

December 1982

Ode to Our Dad
   —on his sixtieth birthday.

It matters not how old you are
When counting up the years.
What really matters most of all
Is that we have you here.

For whether you are sixty
Or whether you are ten,
If health and happiness are yours
Then "age" is still your friend.

And if your most important thoughts
Are not of your own self,
But instead, you're ever striving
To share your earthly wealth

With all mankind around you
Whatever way you can—
With only just a "thank-you"
For lending such a hand—

And if your family is your life,
The Lord your faithful guide,
And maybe one or two close friends
In whom you may confide—

And if it be that Sunday school
Is what you like to teach,
And if it be the homeless poor
Are those you care to reach …

If, too, you have some hobbies
To work in leisure time—
Perhaps a bit of gardening
Or the picture-framing kind—

If one can answer humbly
To what is listed here,
He must truly be a person
Who is loved and held most dear.

For *we* do have this pleasure
In loving such a man—
And our lives are so much richer
Having known his loving hand.

~

February 1983

In the Hearts of Sisters

In the Hearts of Sisters

Once upon a time ago
        I watched two little children grow ...
Two little sisters warm and dear
        Wanting one another near.

They played and fought like fighting friends
        With neither's will about to bend.
It mattered not for running deep
        A loyalty was there for keeps.

They spent their early childhood
        As playful sisters should ...
Playing dolls and make-believe,
        Riding bikes and skinning knees.

And then at night these little girls
        Would share a bed and sweetly curl
Their little bodies soft and warm
        Against each other till the morn.

And when these children blossomed,
        Their loveliness was awesome.
No longer little girls were they
        For womanhood was on its way.

It wouldn't take but just a while
        Until two men would win their smiles.
And then they'd have their separate homes
        While leading lives their very own.

And now although they're miles apart—
        Buried deep within their hearts
The memories of their childhood days
        Are very safely tucked away.

And still the cherished love has stayed
     That long ago those sisters made.
I know them very well, you see …
     For one was you, the other me.

~

April 1983—for love of Janice

My Christening Day

I'm a special little boy child
Very newly born,
And I am being christened
This early Sunday morn.

My mother has a friend who's sewn
A very special gown
That I will very proudly own
And someday pass on down.

How nice if at a future time
I see my own child wear
This pretty little gown of mine
That I would gladly share.

I'm meeting all my relatives
And also many friends.
They come with so much love to give
And precious time to spend.

Indeed, it is a happy day
But solemn too, we know.
For as I'm baptized, all will pray
That in God's grace I'll grow.

I'm sad to think the day must end:
Like me, it needs to sleep—
But hope I do that folks and friends
Will cherish it for keeps.

~

September 1983—for a friend

Ed and Sarah

To you it likely doesn't seem
So very long ago
You stood beside the preacher
To repeat those vows we know.

But it is my opinion
Fifty years is quite a time
To share each other's days and nights
To blend your bodies, souls, and minds.

And so you must feel honored
For it has seemed to me
That God allows but just a few
As many married years as thee.

I can but just imagine
The closeness you possess:
You know the other like yourself,
And love your "other half" the best.

For surely this is what it means
To join and be as one—
To grow in years with strengthened love—
For that is what you two have done!

~

October 1984

To Jan and Bud on Their Fourth Wedding Anniversary

On this your special number four
We come to wish you many more.
And may the closeness that you share
Never ever wane or wear.
And may you both today recall
Those vows you spoke in front of all.

Although the years will come and go
Bringing changes as you grow,
We hope you pledge to always be
From now until eternity
Each other's most important friend,
For then a marriage knows no end.

~

November 1980

Heaven's Most Anxious Baby

I had a home not long ago—
I liked it very much.
It showed so well the view below,
Too far away to touch.

For many long and hopeful years
I thought how nice it'd be
To be allowed to go from here
And journey down to see.

I used to cry when others went;
It somehow wasn't fair.
Always someone else was sent
To spend a while down there.

"It isn't time," is what He'd say,
"Soon, but not just yet."
He promised there would come a day—
And I was not to fret!

But argue on, I would not hush:
Just any spot would do,
And then He said, "I won't be rushed;
I've a special place for you!"

Every day a friend would go;
Another name was called—
I'd watch Him tie the wings just so,
For the little one mustn't fall.

But as the years passed slowly on,
I always wondered why:
Was He sad to have them gone—
For He kissed each little one goodbye?

And then one day I heard Him call—
I thought, "Oh could it be
That maybe, finally, after all
He's not forgotten me?"

The wings He tied that day were mine ...
He gently kissed my brow.
Again, I saw His sadness there:
My time to go was now.

He said I had much joy to bring
To a special place below.
And then I moved my tiny wings—
All set to turn and go ...

When back I looked, I saw Him nod,
Then suddenly I knew:
I'd come again to be with God
But now, I'm to be with you.

~

December 1983—for Janice and Bud, on news of Cole.

Silent Longings

I mourn these human frailties—
Oh, Soul of Mine, do not you see?
Thou knowest all these faults of mine—
Then why not rid me of each kind?

Before I fall asleep, I pray
That I will change by early day.
But all these vows I make myself
I always break on someone else.

Late at night, I'm down the hall
To kneel beside my children small—
And while I watch their peaceful sleep
I often bow my head and weep.

Oh, where is patience in the day
To keep me from the things I say?
And so I vow to try again
To be a better mom to them.

Then, too, I should be kinder still
To him I love and always will.
But then my anger takes a turn
And out come words that cut and burn.

I long to be so poised and calm
To hold the two within my palm.
To never let my feathers fly
And then to see my temper die.

A gentle nature all the time
I'd truly love to say was mine.
At times, I try to copy those
Whose soft and quiet ways I know.

But mostly it is not to be—
For when He shaped and molded me,
All the gentle lambs were gone
And so my purr is lion-strong.

But mourn I do for what can't be,
For every day I'm same old me.
But still I hope a distant time
Will claim a patient side as mine.

~

July 11, 1983 … here's hoping

A Little Girl's Dilemma

I turned around and she was gone—
My little girl of two.
It didn't seem so long ago …
I guess longer than I knew.

Gone are curly pigtails
That couldn't quite keep time
With all her bouncing playfulness.
She's left them all behind.

No more an angel baby face—
Her features, more mature.
Her little body growing—
Womanhood awaiting her.

And lo, she rushes so to be
That woman, fully grown,
To do the things a lady does,
To claim them as her own.

But what a mind and body want
Do sometimes disagree.
Her mind is pushing womanhood;
Her body protests: wait for me!

Then, too, her heart says something else:
"Stay Mommy's little girl—
Be always young and small enough
Upon her lap to curl."

And so my little daughter,
Such a turmoil you are in:
Should you stay the little girl you are?
Or let womanhood begin?

Perhaps if you could maybe take
Each year just one by one,
You'd find that growing up can be
A little bit more fun.

Try not to be so hurried—
Grab onto life and hold.
Don't wish it gone like I once did
When I, too, was only eight years old!

~

February 1984 …for Anna

Relinquishment

Love your child, but let him go;
Don't hold him back with what you know.
We often have to set them free
To find the self they feel to be.

How sad and difficult the task
To let them stray from what you ask.
To see them go upon their way
Ignoring what you have to say.

We bear a child, assign a name,
And quickly in our minds we claim
This child is simply *us* extended—
To think and feel as *we've* intended.

We have to learn a solemn truth:
They are not carbon-copy youths.
Their thoughts and feelings are their own,
And this is what they beg be known.

Oh dear and lovely child of mine—
I gave you life; now help me find
A way, in love, to set you free
To be yourself—not part of me.

February 1985

His Gift of a Child … Our Promise to Keep

How dear and sweet our little Cole—
And oh how much we love you so!
We waited such a time for you—
No doubt, your wait seemed that way, too!
Forgive us if throughout this day
We acted strange in several ways.
Perhaps we hugged and kissed you more—
Or used too much the word "adore."
Today is such a special one
For us and you as well.
Today we stood in front of God
And to Him we did tell
That yes, we know you came from Him—
And only as a loan—
But promised Him that while you're here
You'd be our very own …
That we would take good care of you
And teach you right from wrong
And show you what you ought to do
While helping you along.
But most of all we promised Him
That while you're in our care,
We'd always take the time to spend
To tell you of your God up there.
For He has always loved you so,
And did, but sadly, let you go,
While giving us the stern command
To take you by your little hand
And teach you well, about His love
And of His Heaven there above.
He wants to be assured that when
He calls back home, John Cole …
That you will know the way to Him,
Remembering Him of old.
So this is called your Christening Day,
A special day indeed:

For we have stood in faith to say
We'll do our best to lead
This child, so newly come from Thee,
To live a Christian Way,
Remembering all the while God's plea:
He must come back, someday, to Me.

~

November 1984—to Cole with love

Inwardly Speaking
For Meghan

You came to us when God stepped in
And said we weren't to question Him,
But that He wanted you to *be*—
So now, today, you're part of me.

In truthfulness, it took some time
To comprehend that you were mine.
For many moons have risen high
Since last I sang a lullaby.

But on the day you leave this mold,
When then I see I'm not too old,
The joy I felt each birth before
I know I'll feel, again, once more.

So fear you not, my little one,
For in the spring the day will come
When I will hold you close to me
And you will feel my love for thee.

And in a cradle you will sleep,
While Mommy tries her best to keep
Her tears of wondrous love, somehow
From tumbling down upon your brow.

But as of now, you're still so small—
The time of year is only fall.
The dreary days of winter months
Must pass before you're born to us.

And so, my sweet, I pray to Him
Who planted you so deep within,
That every day will mean to you
The perfect growth of something new.

And I will do my very best
To keep you safe inside your nest.
We'll work together still as one
Till nature says our job is done.

And on the day that you are born
They'll wrap you up to keep you warm.
And when they lay you by my side
Once more, I'll hum a lullaby!

~

October 1985—we love you, little one.

Waiting

I'm waiting ... still, I'm waiting
For this baby to be born.
And now with every passing day,
My strength is further worn.

I'm still awake at early dawn
When day breaks forth with light ...
For sleeplessness has surely been
My foe throughout these nights.

Of late, I cannot seem to find
For even just a while
A way to ease my weary self
While heavy with this child.

How good when I can hold it close,
And feel its face on mine—
To see our separateness complete
After all these months entwined.

Indeed, it is a miracle—
This child alive in me—
And how our God has made it grow,
But it's time to set it free.

It used to be exciting
To have this babe within—
But now we're both exhausted
And wanting nature to begin.

Oh patience, do not leave me—
Do not forsake me now.
In just a week, my baby
Is supposed to take its bow.

But worry has engulfed me:
Suppose it should be late?
How then to cope with all of this
And endure the added wait?

But in a book that I just read
Some words did speak to me—
They said, "Wait you, upon the Lord,
And He will strengthen thee."

And thus, I was reminded—
Since my God did plant within
This tiny child some months ago
And made this all begin—

That He's also planned the hour
That He wishes it to end,
And all I have to do is wait
Till He looks my way again.

And with His nod, my time will come:
My baby will be born.
For He has planned it all along,
And I needn't feel forlorn.

~

April, 1986—one week left before our third child is due to be born.

My Song to Meghan Laurel
   (Sung to the tune of "Happy Birthday")

Meghan Laurel are you
      A daughter and sister, too.
You came to us unexpectedly;
      Now we're glad you're one of the family.

Momma loved you yesterday,
      Momma loves you today.
Momma loves you tomorrow,
      Momma loves you always.

You're the sweetest thing I've seen,
      You're the sweetest thing I know,
You're sweet as a dream,
      And I love you so.

I pray for you a long life—
      Full of happiness, no strife.
May all your dreams come true,
      May God be with you.

~

May 1986—newborn baby Meggie

Mutual Affection

He walks with her and talks with her
And gently calls her name.
She smiles and calls him "Dada";
Then begs to play a game.

She shows him all her many books,
Her little dolls and such.
She's young and so her words are few,
Yet she knows she loves him much.

He wraps her up and takes her out
To play awhile outdoors—
She runs and romps about her world
Following him, who she adores.

So often, she dislikes her crib
So he takes her to our bed.
She proudly wears a victory grin;
Then gently lays her head.

A mother's love's instinctual—
Expected from the start.
A father's love, however,
Must grow within his heart.

A child responds to love received,
And when all is said and done,
How great it is if Daddy's love
And baby's love are one.

~

January 1988—for love of CM and Meghan

Awakening Cries

Little baby, why this cry?
Such tears upon your face.
Saddened eyes and choking sighs,
Your precious smile you waste.

Perhaps a frightening dream
Where friend did turn to foe,
Where light turned into darkness,
Or you fell while on the go.

Perhaps you woke and missed me
And feared that I was gone.
Come baby into Momma's arms;
I've been here all along.

~

April 1988

Quiet Child

Not much to say, this quiet child:
Very shy, her manner mild.
But deep within her gentle soul
Lie thoughts that few will ever know.

Part of every day alone,
But still insists it's hers to own.
Repeatedly, she says she's fine—
A happy, saddened child entwined.

Her fate to be with older ones,
A plight that cannot be undone.
And yet she bravely still survives,
This lovely younger, older child.

And yet at times, a sadness comes
Upon her face. One asks where from?
But often never answers, she,
Except to turn and walk from thee.

Retreating thus unto herself,
She simply answers no one else.
Only she can really know
From whence her sadness comes and goes.

But often times, when one-on-one,
She blooms and shines, becomes the sun.
Her smile is wide, her humor long,
Convincing you she does belong.

As sensitive as one can be,
She really truly wants to please.
Thankful for the least of things,
But most of all, the love you bring.

Her loveliness is quickly seen,
But truer beauty has always been
From early on and all the while
Within the heart of this quiet child.

~

April 1988—for love of Meghan

Familiar Call

I've never been too popular;
This trait I cannot claim.
But every time I turn around,
I seem to hear my name!

•

At times, I think I'm all alone—
There's just the gentle rain.
I think I've found a quiet place,
     (But wait!)
I think I heard my name!

•

I'm busy doing housework—
My routine is just the same:
Stop and start, then stop again,
     (Oh, no!)
Someone's called my name!

•

I'm working in the kitchen—
To cook is such a pain,
And then to make this matter worse,
     (Great day!)
Again there goes my name!

•

I'm talking on the phone
To a friend who feels the same;
Ten times we're interrupted—
     (You guessed!)
Someone knows our names!

•

There's fighting in my midst
And also shouts of blame—
I know it won't be long
     (That's right!)
Before I'll hear my name!

•

I try to take a bath
With privacy my aim;
Then simply out of nowhere—
        (Once more!)
A voice has called my name!
                •

Alas, real late at night,
I admit with certain shame
How nice the peace and quiet
        (Indeed!)
When no one says my name!
                •

I'm seldom called by Mrs.
Or Ms. or any other—
I mostly answer to the sound
Of little voices calling- …
        MO-THER!

~

November 1987

Sisters Three

Bonded by blood
And bonded by love,
These sisters three
Were destined to be.
Their love undefined,
Without limits of time.
Beyond simple caring,
Confiding and sharing,
Unparalleled joy
These sisters employ.

They'd battle mankind,
These daughters of mine,
To save one another
Or outsmart their mother!
Like cats in the night,
They scheme and they fight.
But strangers beware;
They're quickly prepared
To fight to the end
If an outsider offends.

Their rule is but one:
There better be none
Who even would dare
Harm a sister of theirs.
Each others' best friends,
They often do lend
A shoulder to lean
When someone's been mean.

Warm bodies in bed
Curled head to head,
They ward off the ghosts
That each fears the most.
They plan and they dream;
They plot and they scheme,
Mapping out days
In set little ways.
How precious and sweet
Their love, let it keep.

May always there be
These beautiful three.
Three little sisters ...
Three daughters for me.

~

January 1988

Heavy Hearts

Her heart is heavy; her soul is sad—
Let something come to make her glad.
Forbid her cry this freezing morn
Waiting for the bus, forlorn:
Heated words on broken rules
Just before she left for school.
The fault was clearly hers to bear,
But let a friend her sorrow share.
Remind her, Lord, we love her well;
Restore the ego, too, that fell.
It pains my heart to see her so;
When home she comes, I'll let her know.
Lord, help refrain our stubborn wills
And make tomorrow better still.

~

February 1988—for love of Melanie

Easter in the Park

She saw him on a yonder bench,
A sadness in his eyes.
She wandered for a closer look
And caught him by surprise.

He deeply frowned and snapped away,
"Who be I to you?
What right you have to come o'er here
And stare at what I do?"

Indeed, he surely frightened her,
A little girl of three.
"I'm sorry if I angered you,"
So shyly answered she.

"I saw you sitting over here
And thought I'd say hello.
Instead, I guess I bothered you,
So I guess I better go."

"Come back here, little runt
And sit wi'me a while."
She did so, willingly,
Hoping he would smile.

"Where been you little girl;
Where be your Ma 'bout now?"
"I've been huntin' Easter eggs
And lost my way somehow."

"See my pretty basket—
I found a awful lot.
I come to give you some.
Would you like a egg or not?"

"They be no good to me—
Them eggs be just for kids.
How come your Ma ain't frantic,
Runnin' off the way you did?"

"Oh, she'll be plenty mad …
And scared, I reckon too.
But I will tell my momma
That I made friends with you."

"My daddy has a job.
He goes to work all day.
Aren't you lonely, mister,
Sitting here this way?"

"I ain't so lucky, child;
No work that I can do.
Haven't any friends,
Exceptin' maybe you."

She gathered up her eggs
And turned towards the man.
"I think I see my mom,"
Then touched his feeble hand.

"Little girl, but wait—
I think I changed me mind:
One of them there eggs
I'd like to say is mine."

The little girl was happy
With her friend of just a while.
Holding out her basket
He took an egg, and smiled.

She quickly turned to go,
Her mom had grabbed her hand.
Turning back, she yelled to him,
"Happy Easter, Mister Man!"

~

April 1988

The Friends

She was different from her friend—
Different homes and different schools.
Their moms were even different,
Setting forth quite different rules.

To the one, sophistication
Was important to attain.
To the other, it was something
She didn't care she couldn't claim.

They didn't wear the same in clothes,
Nor share each other's friends.
Their hobbies even differed:
One took dancing, one took gym.

There were different graduations,
And then careers pursued.
But always they did keep in touch
And so their friendship grew.

When marriages and children
Led them far away from here,
They worried that their friendship
Might wane and disappear.

Indeed their lives had changed;
There were happy times and sad.
But neither girl forgot
The childhood friend she had.

And then one day they visited—
In past, they only called.
And both were overjoyed—
Each hadn't changed at all.

One was very worldly,
The other *quiet town.*
And still they got along
Despite their differences around.

They marveled at the irony
That many times a friend
They had so much in common with
Was here and gone again.

And yet these two together,
So different from the start,
Sat across from one another
And knew within their hearts

They would love each other always;
Their friendship had endured.
And now they knew for certain
They were friends for life for sure.

~

April 1988 ---for Allison and Anna

Mary

She was honored today
In a real loving way
With a gathering here
Of friends she holds dear.

Church peers have met
Voting not to forget
All the hours she's spent
Of herself that she's lent.

The list is too long
Of the deeds that belong
To lie by her name—
But they'll try just the same.

And so they've confided
And in secret decided
Their love they would show
Through this honor bestowed.

I also know well
Of this woman I tell.
Though friend to those others,
I claim her as mother.

And all that they've said
Tonight in her stead
I know in my heart
She's earned from the start.

Still yet there is more
Not recognized for—
Great virtues unstated,
Unlisted, undated.

Her bravery through pain,
She doesn't complain,
Maintaining appearance
With great perseverance.

Her listening powers
By the minute or hour ...
A friend always there
And waiting to care.

Armed with compassion
And able to ration
Her love among many,
To give it to any.

So quick to say yes
To offer her best
With laughter or tears
To strangers or peers.

Grandmother to four,
And each she adores.
They, too, with a yearn
Love back in return.

There's also a man—
Most loyal of fans.
The love of his life—
This lady, his wife.

Let us honor her well,
This woman who dwells
As a model to others:
My friend and my mother.

~

September 1989—for love of Mom

Ballad of the Angels

There once were two angels in Heaven,
And each was the other's best friend.
Though young, they played happily together,
Till suddenly it came to an end.

The little boy angel was given
His long awaited-for wings.
'Twas sad the day that they parted—
For surely they'd play not again.

In tears, the little girl angel
Unhappily kissed him good-bye.
A couple below had begged for a babe—
And God said, "Yes, my boy, go fly!"

The angel longed to be grateful;
He'd waited and dreamed of today.
Why had he never considered
That his birth would send him away?

He wished to take her along also,
Thus keeping her safe at his side.
But alas, she wasn't invited;
Only one little babe could survive.

But surely, it couldn't be over—
Would fate reunite them again?
"Dear God," they desperately pleaded,
"Remember how long we've been friends."

Soon after, the angel departed
And was born to an earthly pair.
Though greatly loved and tended
He yearned for his friend up There.

And she in turn grew lonely;
The angels whispered low,
"Her little heart's been broken
Since he left a year ago."

And even God grew worried;
He anguished at her tears.
In time He soon decided
To send her far from Here.

"Come hither, little angel."
She flew to His command.
"Be comforted, My little one,
For I have come upon a plan."

"Not long ago I heard a prayer—
A woman seeking three.
Two children has she now—
How 'bout I send her thee?

"It would mean you'd have two sisters,
Much older, yes I know.
But see do I great joy and love,
So I'm asking you to go."

"I accept," replied the angel,
Though fearful, yet she knew
That God would never let her down—
So off away she flew.

Getting born was somewhat harder
Than she'd expected it to be.
And more than ever, she was wanting
Her angel friend to see.

She was sure she'd never find him—
God had made the earth too vast.
So she guessed their loving friendship
Would stay forever in the past.

A couple of years were over,
And Angel Boy was two.
"I really love it here," he thought,
"Except for missing you."

He'd not forget his angel,
And his search would never end:
Always babies being born—
Somewhere he'd find his friend.

Not long beyond his birthday,
His mother cuddled close
And said she had some happy news
That should really please them both.

Her sister had a baby girl,
A cousin she would be—
"And later when she's bigger,
She can play with little me?"

"Today we'll go to visit,"
His mom continued on.
"It will take us several hours,
And the journey will be long."

"Please remember, sweetheart,
As yet, she's very small.
It will still be quite a while
Before she'll play at all."

Her little angel listened,
But it tickled so his wings.
For his mother didn't understand:
"We angels know these things!"

They arrived to see the baby;
She was soft and pink and sweet.
But the little angel boy
Was shocked with disbelief ...

There lying in a bassinet
Asleep … his angel friend!
And thus his long and desperate search
Was coming to an end.

She stirred and opened wide her eyes
And seeing no one else,
She saw her unforgotten friend—
'Twas truly he himself!

Then softly laughter filled the room;
They said how cute we were.
"If they could know our story
They'd think us sweet for sure!"

His anxious soul was waiting
To sneak inside her room.
And be again with her he loved
To lift their parted gloom.

With everybody occupied
And sure he'd not be missed—
At last beside her bassinet
Her sleeping face he kissed.

His pounding heart awakened her;
Her smile revealed her joy.
Unknowing how—but there he stood,
Her beloved angel boy.

They talked in angel language,
Though not a word was said.
He told of his adventures,
Of the search for her he'd led.

She told how great her loneliness
Had been without him near;
How God had then decided
He'd better send her here.

"What a great coincidence,"
She pondered to her friend—
"That our parents know each other
And can visit now and then."

At that, he gave a chuckle,
Then explained it from the start ...
"And so you see we're cousins;
Thus, we'll never be apart!"

"But wait, I do remember ..."
Then suddenly she smiled—
"God had said He had a plan.
Guess He planned *this* all the while!"

And thus the little angels,
Reunited once again,
Can now through all eternity
Remain each other's friend.

~

February 1989—for love of Cole and Meg

A Child's Christmas

A Child's Christmas

To view another Christmas
Through the eyes of children small,
To feel their wonder and excitement
Over anything at all.

To live again the marvel
When first you saw a tree,
Unbelieving of its beauty,
In your house for all to see.

"Look Momma at the angel",
(Sitting high upon the branch),
"And all the lights are twinkling
Like a ballerina dance".

Then, too, the decorations
In the home, the stores, the street …
So great his fascination,
"Can I touch them please?" he squeaks.

The aromas known to Christmas,
Rich with cinnamon and spice,
The little child is asking
"What smells so sweet and nice?"

And on that day of baking
Those cookies, pies, and breads,
A toddler comes a'begging
For that cookie "dressed in red"!

And every night, they go to bed—
Such questions in their eyes!
"Do you really think he'll bring
That doll that blinks and cries?"

How incredible the fantasy—
A jolly bearded man
Making toys and raising reindeer
In a snowy, distant land,

Who visits every little child
Real late on Christmas Eve,
Leaving dolls and trucks and bikes
To all who still believe.

Then off he rides upon his sleigh,
His reindeer at the head.
And leaving every house, he waves
To those all tucked in bed.

In the midst, each mother tries
To tell of long ago:
"One Christmas Day a babe was born
And His name you need to know."

So thus beside each Christmas tree
There lays a manger scene
In hopes that little children
Will learn what Christmas means.

But think I do it must be hard
For one so small to see
The joy of Someone's birthday
With those presents 'neath the tree!

And yet surprised we moms have been
When Christmas Eve is done,
When Santa's notes are written
And his snack left out in fun,

When then we tuck our toddler in,
His mind a blur of toys,
We thrill to hear him whisper low,
"Happy Birthday, Jesus boy"!

~

November 1989

The Rose and the Weed

Fidelity, a rose or weed
Nursed, neglected, like flower seeds,
Each is planted. Someone's toil—
One seeks the soul, the other soil.

For some, a solemn pledge pursued,
A promise made to not abuse
A holy vow. And like the rose,
With nurturing, it blooms and grows.

But what of dreams so slyly stilled,
A promise made but not fulfilled?
Neglected like forgotten weeds—
Uncaring of another's needs.

And thus, we choose which road to walk—
Both ways of life await our knock.
But lo, beside the blooming rose
There thrives the weed. So close, it grows.

~

February 1990

The Farm

The Farm

We'd awaken very early
To a crisp and cloudy morn,
Serenaded by the rooster
Proclaiming day was born.

Down the stairs we hurried
And hid behind the door
To glimpse the milk truck in the lane—
'Twas what we'd wakened for.

Two sisters on a farm were we,
That June, my fifteenth year,
And one embarrassed milk boy
Who saw us crouching near.

Unlimited adventures
Awaited, to be found
On that quaint old country farm
By a graveled road near town.

Back then, there stood a henhouse
Not far behind the barn.
And off I'd go a'fetching
With a basket round my arm.

A welcomed change for city girls,
This quiet, peaceful pace,
A taste of independence
Far from home, this charming place.

Enchanted by those piglets
And their frantic little squeals
Who fought to find a place at trough
For yet another meal.

Special were the days we planned
To drive to town for lunch—
In pickup truck with dog along—
A carefree happy bunch.

So quaint that country coffee shop—
I hope it stands today.
Indeed, 'tis reminiscent
Of times since passed away.

How dear to us the lady
Who lived and worked the farm,
Inviting us each summer
To come enjoy its charms.

While treating us like daughters,
This childless aunt of ours
Helped weave for us the memories
Now blooming sweet as flowers.

No more a girl, a woman now
With children quite a few—
But time can never fade or mar
That farm that once I knew.

~

December 1990

Love Revisited

The road they walked upon this earth
While joined as man and wife
Slowly headed downward
Throughout their married life.

Spoken words too often cruel
Were better left unsaid;
And those that could have comforted
Were never voiced instead.

Loving gestures long denied,
Compassion just a phrase,
Laughter seldom visited
Their often solemn days.

But somewhere buried deep within
The love that first was theirs,
Though now but just a memory,
'Twas all they had to share.

And then one died. And left behind
A lonely grieving soul,
Lost without the partner
Who had shared their love grown cold.

For many years, the one survived,
Perhaps in deep regret,
That neither found a way to save
What was felt when first they met.

But far too late to change the past
These lonely years have shown
Perhaps their love went deeper
Than either one had known.

And now this poor and wretched soul
Has breathed a tired sigh
And gone to meet the soul mate
From days long since gone by.

Maybe they'll be kinder,
More caring to each other,
Since now they both have known the loss
Of one without the other.

Within the miracles of Heaven,
Born anew by holy breath,
Perhaps their love will flourish,
If not in life, in death.

~

October 1994

The Sacrifice

They were playing in the ocean,
A mother and her sons.
A warm and sultry summer's day,
A bit of harmless fun.

Too suddenly, it happened,
Not a warning nor a sign—
Like an undersea tornado
It sucked them out in little time.

The older boy was strongest,
Pulling free—his mom implored
That he try to swim to safety,
So he headed back to shore.

Vowing he would save them both,
Yet his race for help was slow—
Exhausted by his struggle
And still so far to go.

Her little one was floundering,
Too young to hold his own.
He couldn't tread the water
Nor could he float alone.

She knew the chance was very slim
That help would come in time.
To save her son from drowning,
She would leave herself behind.

She'd put him on her shoulders
And show him how to clap
The water with his little hands
And stay afloat like that.

She'd be underneath the water
And would fight to hold her breath,
But she would die so he could live—
It was all that she had left.

In tears, she kissed her son good-bye
And trying to be brave
She placed him on her shoulders,
Then slipped beneath the waves.

The rescue team was summoned
By the son who swam to shore.
Arriving out to sea, they found
His little brother, only four.

He was clapping at the water
And sobbing, yet alive.
Too late to save their mother—
She had known she'd not survive.

In dying, she had given life,
No greater one can be.
Her sons are living tributes
To that choice she made at sea.

~

April 1993—in memory of the woman who did this.

Patterns Repeated

Momma's busy; run along.
I haven't time to hear your song.
Perhaps another day will do,
A better time to hear you through.

Momma's busy, not today.
I mustn't stop; I can't delay.
Try again another time
If then you see a minute's mine.

Momma's busy; hurry on.
Tomorrow we will plan your prom.
Tomorrow we will buy your gown.
Today, however, chores abound.

Momma's busy; beg me not
To call it quits and early stop.
I know your wedding's soon to be;
We'll get it done, I promise thee.

Momma's rested. Done at last.
Now I've time to sit and laugh.
Recite those stories sweet and dear
The ones I hadn't time to hear.

Momma's lonely; let me come
And baby-sit your precious son.
My, but how you're on the go—
Every day you hurry so.

Momma's puzzled, saddened too—
What happened to the child I knew?
My little girl is fully grown,
Hurried days now hers to own.

Momma sheds a silent tear,
Shakes her head at what she hears—
Those ancient phrases loosely said
Now her daughter says instead:

Momma's busy; run along.
I haven't time to hear your song.
Another day, my little son,
When Momma isn't on the run.

~

October 1992

The Phone Call

She shyly dials his number,
Her pounding heart a drum.
If he answers, will she falter—
Will her voice be just a hum?

'Twas he who called her last,
Suggesting she call him.
Still, awkwardness is with them
As their friendship just begins.

Perhaps he won't be home—
Disappointment or relief?
Should she dare to leave a message
Or hang up in disbelief?

Perhaps his mom will answer,
Or even worse, his dad.
What then? she faintly wonders.
Where's the confidence she had?

Maybe nonchalant
Is the way she'll try to sound.
Should she say she isn't busy—
Has he seen the show in town?

Maybe he'll be grumpy,
Unmoved to sit and chat.
If she mumbles something stupid,
Will he hang up just like that?

How well I do remember
These painful times of teens.
I'd rather be her mother
Than still be chasing dreams.

I think perhaps he's answered—
Her voice is soft and slow.
I peer around the corner
As she meekly asks "Hel-lo?"

~

June 1994—for "Poor Mellie"

Heartbreak

They fought. Using harsh and hurtful words,
Each pounding out the other; and then in pain they heard
A declaration it was over. With angry hearts and tears
They cried and cursed the dial tone that was left for each to hear.

Two people come together; their lives are intertwined,
And for a while, their bonding is so totally aligned.
Their love is all-consuming; they think of little else;
They dream and scheme of when to meet and see the other's self.

They lean on one another; their secrets have no end.
They are confidants and lovers, each other's cherished friend.
They analyze and fantasize, so sure that all is well,
Convinced that nothing mortal could ever break their spell.

Adoring looks, endearing names, they devour one another;
Their playfulness is tossed from one unto the other.
It doesn't matter what they do or how they spend their time,
Just being close together is all they have in mind.

And then one day it happens; they argue on the phone.
The silent, painful aftermath, without the other—so alone...
Unbearable, unthinkable, yet still they argue on,
And with every conversation, paint out the other's wrongs.

One still loves the other; the other loves him back,
But both are just as stubborn and refuse to take the rap.
And so they wait and ponder, their pride the biggest sin,
But at the sound of every phone, they pray,
"I hope it's her." "I hope it's him."

~

February 1996—for Melanie

Choices of Love

Within her heart, she loves them both,
These two from different worlds.
And they in turn have each confessed
Their love for this same girl.

For one, a simple country boy,
Content to stay at home—
Not tempted by a world beyond
The roots from which he's grown.

The city boy, with packaged plans
Of where his life should go,
Has plotted for himself a course
To follow as he goes.

Ironic how they differ so
Yet share a common thread,
For both are captivated by
The other's girl instead.

Born and raised a city girl,
But country now is home.
Capable of either life—
The choice is hers alone.

Deeply loved; in love with them,
Confusion frets her mind,
Saddened by the knowledge that
She must leave a love behind.

One she'll choose to stand beside
On that holiest of days,
But all the while knowing
Within her soul, the other stays.

~

September 1995

If Only

If only I could ease your pain
And wipe away your tears,
To see you never frown again
And keep you safely near.

If only I could show you how
To solve your every woe,
Erasing thus your furrowed brow
While troubles swiftly go.

If only I could keep you strong
For that which comes your way,
And help you choose each right and wrong
Throughout your busy day.

If only I could keep you safe
And ward off every harm
Before it has the chance to chafe
Or interrupt your charm.

If only I could see you laugh
And hear it echo long,
And know 'twas not for my behalf
You sang your happy song.

If only I could send you love
Beyond my very own,
Whatever kind you're dreaming of,
The kind you ache to know.

If only I could do all these
And see your face aglow.
For then, in turn, you'd clearly see
How much I love you so.

~

September 1993—for love of my three girls.

Miniature Mom

Go ahead and make me small
And stuff me in your bag.
Take me with you where you go,
And that will make me glad.
Perch me up atop your shoulders,
So I can ride along—
Whisper to me now and then,
And I'll whisper back a song.
Take me out when you're afraid
And know that I am near.
Show me what is frightening you,
So I can whisk away your fears.
Tell me all your happy thoughts;
Keep me close when you are sad.
I'm small enough to blow away
Every tear you've ever had.
Dance with me around your room,
But be careful I don't drop.
I love to see you laughing—
Let your dancing never stop.
And when it's time to tuck you in,
To rest your sleepy head,
Make me just a little bigger
So we can snuggle in your bed.

~

October 1999

Woman on the Rise

Beautiful, yet serious,
Her sights set straight ahead.
Her plans are all mapped out
And underlined in red.

She can answer many questions
And figure things right out.
Common sense—her constant friend—
That's what she's all about.

She's sensitive and caring
And hopeful to the end.
Strong and quite supportive—
She can stand against the wind.

Constant and consistent,
And honest through and through.
She simply tells you like it is,
And you can bet it to be true.

Determined in her choices
To achieve her long-term goals—
Second best will only do
If a plan is put on hold.

A lovely girl, her future bright,
A sparkle in her eyes.
With life stretched out before her,
She's a woman on the rise!

~

November 1998—for love of Melanie

Love(ly) as a Leaf

Newfound love is like the leaf
When just a bud in early spring.
Young and still so innocent,
A tender, cherished, fragile thing.

Once summer comes, the leaf has bloomed,
And hanging steadfast from its tree,
It matures to show its splendor,
But still a complex thing to see.

Then comes the autumn season,
And the leaf, full in its prime,
So proud of all its color,
Still stands the test of time.

But soon the leaf grows weary
And tumbles far below
Still it well remembers
When it glowed not long ago.

Now nestled in a quiet place—
Indeed 'tis not its tree—
But winter snows are peaceful
And the leaf is free to be.

~

January 1999

Legend of the Lovers

She stood by herself, graceful as a deer,
High on a hill, quite a ways from here.
The wind blew her hair like the leaves of a tree,
And her flowing white dress lifted high in the breeze.

Quite sure I was safe and hadn't been seen—
Then suddenly she turned and peered down at me.
Struck by her splendor, I froze in my place,
While desperately trying to make out her face.

Approaching fog quickly made its way in,
And that night, I did not see her again.
From whence she came or where she went—
Did she come on her own or perhaps was she sent?

The following night and those that came after,
She stood on her hill, still, without laughter.
She never smiled, nor spoke a word,
Yet the voice of her soul surely I heard.

I dared not approach, nor did she descend—
I feared that in knowing, it might come to an end.
An angel, a ghost, or perhaps even real—
I no longer cared, for she had taught me to feel.

And so we have loved every night from afar,
Neither of us knowing who we both really are.
Having not ever touched, having not ever spoken,
Yet our hearts are as one—free and wide open…

And so legend would have it, they continued their love
Till a bolt of lightning struck down from above.
And while killing them both, their souls became sewn;
Thus, the truths of each other at last to be known.

That night they ascended to the heavens on high,
And while joyously laughing, they entered the sky.
The legend has said there are two stars that embrace—
The girl on the hill and her love, face to face.

~

July 1998

Chance Meeting

She drove forward to the window
To withdraw a bit of cash.
Just a routine, simple errand—
On her list, it was the last.

He walked in, approached the counter
To deposit needed cash.
Just a routine, simple errand—
On his list, it was the last.

She looked in and started grinning,
So familiar was this man.
And casting out embarrassment
She started waving with her hand.

He looked up and started grinning,
He had known her long in life.
And casting out embarrassment
He waved back toward his wife!

~

February 1988

The Highway Man

He drives these busy highways
Without failure every week.
Same old roads, same old signs,
And always in the driver's seat.

He loads his truck and turns the key
And off, away he goes;
A very long and lonely drive
This boring route he knows.

He plays his favorite radio
To pass this awful time.
I wonder if he hums along,
This highwayman of mine.

I know his thoughts control the wheel,
While speeding on his way.
I'm hoping that he thinks of me,
As I think of him today.

This drive he does is out of love,
To work and back to home—
Providing those within his care
His very best, and all alone.

He's home for now, but not for long,
Too soon the day will come
When back inside his truck he'll go—
His weekend said and done.

~

February 1999—for love of and deep gratitude to C.M.—a wonderful
and loving husband and father!

No Regrets

What if she'd married someone else?
She ponders to herself.
What if he had wed another?
They'd each be someone else.
If given time, and time enough,
They both begin to mold
Each one unto the other
As their lives together grow.
One day they wake and find themselves
Unlike the way they were
So very many years ago—
Because of him? Because of her?
What lives were never found? she asks,
Because they both had met.
But what about the life they've made—
One she'd choose to not forget.
Churning water under bridges,
Many unpaved, bumpy roads.
Too much time thus spent together
To ever think of letting go.
We each can claim our lost and founds
And think of those we never met—
But years become a history
And I have surely no regrets.

~

September 1988

The Farm House

A small and country farmhouse
I'll turn it into home.
I'll make it come alive
When we move out there alone.

The walls adorned with pictures
The windows dressed as well.
And every piece of furniture
Will bring a memory to tell.

All my country nicknacks
Will force the house to bloom.
And there will be a quaintness
To every single room.

The gas logs burning brightly
Will warm this cozy spot,
And we will gather round its hearth
To feel the homeyness it's brought.

The kitchen will be small,'tis true
But charming, you will see.
And round the kitchen table
We'll sit and talk, we three.

And on the porch, a country swing
To watch the passersby;
Surrounded by a picket fence
To mark the place where we reside.

And then in certain corners
My wind chimes will be hung
So we can hear them singing
When the wind begins to hum.

A simple country life I plan
With cows beyond the barn.
And late into the darkened night
The owl surveys our farm.

I've heard him many times before
And I'm sure that he approves.
It is good that we decided
To be brave and make this move.

~

January 1999

Perfect Moment

On my little white swing on my lovely white porch
I sit and listen to the falling rain.
Sheltered by eight leafy trees
That keep my yard from looking plain.

My grass is mowed, the clipping's done,
My sidewalk's lined with stones.
My wind chime sings when the breeze stirs by
As I contentedly swing alone.

I hear the roosters up the street
While cars are whizzing by!
And even so my rowdy dog
Seems content to quiet lie.

The cows are way up in the ridges,
The barns are empty, standing still.
And in the quickly darkening dusk
The birds still chirp in evening's chill.

I've just now turned my porch lights on—
They cast a soft and subtle glow
Reflecting thus an inner calm
This lovely time has let me know.

A little bit of perfectness
In a not so perfect world.
And so I'll try to savor long
This hour, pure and pearled.

~

June 1999

Left Behind

I've left my Blue Ridge Parkway
For a sprawling cattle farm.
And yes, I miss the way those mountains
Unfold their loving arms.

I still have mountains round me
And rolling ridges all my own.
But I miss the way the Parkway
Curved right around our home.

I love our new and small abode,
The peace within its hills,
The cattle grazing here and yon—
But I miss the Parkway still.

I planned our quaint and charming house,
'Tis country through and through.
But the road beyond my doorstep
Is not the Parkway I once knew.

And when the memories strike a chord
And my soul begins to sigh
I run high into my ridges
To keep from asking why.

And there I find the answer:
That all this land is *mine* ...
But the gently curving Parkway
Is forever owned by time.

~

August 1999—for the Blue Ridge Parkway

Forgive Me, Forgive Me Not

I want to say a thousand sorries
For this monstrous thing I've done:
I moved you from the house you loved,
And I know you still feel stunned.

I think you fairly like it here—
'Twas you who bought this land.
But moving from our dream house
Was not what you had planned.

I know you miss the spaciousness,
The large, wide opened rooms.
And all the picture windows
That provided countless views.

You miss the higher, quiet loft
That housed your desk and things,
And all the peaceful privacy
That such a room can bring.

Then, too, the sight of new mown grass,
A yard that *you* had groomed;
A creek that *you* had tended,
And trees that *you* had pruned.

You knew you were a part of
A legendary trail,
And you built above a Parkway
Whose beauty never fails.

A farm you bought while very young
That symbolized your youth.
A farm you thought you'd age with
And never dreamed you'd lose.

How could I have done this—
Pursuing such a thought?
How ever will I really know—
Have you forgiven me or not?

~

September 1999

The Request

He had fallen in love for a second time
Never plotting or planning that her he would find.
Nor had he wished it would ever occur:
In love as he was with the wife he'd adored.

Without any warning, she was suddenly there
And surprisingly so, he found that he cared.
Revealing the truth to his wife, who was shocked,
She asked him to leave and bolted the lock.

Soon after, he learned that his lover was ill
And determined to stay and love her until …
He asked of his wife could he go for awhile
To be with his other through difficult trials.

And when it was over, he'd want to return
To be with his wife where his passion still burned.
She gave him his leave and bid him good-bye,
Angry and heartsick, for days she would cry.

His lover lived on a few months and was gone,
And he aimlessly wandered, just getting along.
Till finally he made his way to her door
And begged to come home like it all was before.

But the time apart had forced her to be
Independent and strong, successfully free.
She said it was over; it would no longer work.
She had dealt with the tears and conquered the hurt.

Her life had gone on although he had left,
Now his turn had come to deal with the rest.
The grief was now his, the aloneness in life,
For thus he had neither: not lover nor wife.

February 1999

A Boy's Grief

He turns and tosses, he cannot sleep,
Something is missing across his feet.
His pillow is empty, a barren spot—
Something was there that loved him a lot.

A buddy, a pet, a boy's best friend,
A mutual love till the bitter end.
One could talk, the other not,
But the other's company each had sought.

One would dare to spill his soul,
The other, quiet, seemed to know
Instinctively just what to do
To cheer the friend he greatly knew.

On cold and boring, rainy days
The two would find a way to play.
Each would seek the other out
To see what they could be about.

Always near each other's side
Kindred spirits by and by.
For one to lose the other one
Would mean a darkened day had come.

And so it has. His grief is great—
He's lost the friend he had of late.
His little pal through thick and thin
Was sadly called away from him.

And now each night he goes to bed
Without his buddy by his head.
A broken heart lies down to sleep,
And silently his momma weeps.

~

November 1999—for love of Cole and his Cozy

Strong Survivor

What was once a lonely year
Has now become eleven—
An eternity of flashbacks
Since he left and went to heaven.
A strong and quiet, sturdy soul,
The wife he left behind.
She braved her grief and held her tears
And pretended she'd be fine.
Eleven years, so long a time,
Days and nights to be alone,
And yet she bravely carries on
In the house they called their home.
She doesn't let you see her cry,
Indeed 'tis not her style—
But still you know she's hurting
Deep down and all this while.
She's seen a lot of changes
In the family she holds so dear,
And I know with every single one
She's wished that he were here.
I fear a day might sadly come
When in her shoes I'll be—
But I can only hope that I'll
Be half as strong as she.

~

June 1999—for love of Beulah

The Present

Unto her, he gave a present,
One she'd never had before—
So elegant and beautiful,
To be cherished ever more.

And with the present, came a card:
Written lines she'd never heard.
Sincerity and gratitude
Expressed in his own words.

He wrote of things he'd never said,
Things she'd often longed to hear.
He humbly sat before her
As she read his words so dear.

He'll never fully understand
The present's total wealth—
He knows he gave a lovely gift,
But to her, he gave himself.

On many grand occasions,
It will sparkle round her throat,
But every day within her heart,
She will wear the words he wrote.

January 2000—for love of C.M.

Him

You've loved a person half your life
And you belong to only him.
He's taught you half of what you know,
Since he robbed your cradle then.

You think you're independent
And free as any bird,
But still in all reality
His voice is all you've heard.

And so you often ponder
How on earth you'd get along.
Without his constant guidance,
Your life would soon go wrong.

Whoever would you cry to,
Who would listen to your tales,
Whoever would you trust again
When you knew he never failed?

No one knows you like he does
Or accepts just who you are.
He helps you understand yourself
And nails it right on par!

He's a wizard with our money;
He's better than the best,
But if left to my own devices,
I know I'd make a mess.

He gives advice to all the girls,
With plans for each concern.
I fear that I would fail them
On issues I never learned.

And so I must concede defeat—
The answers come again,
And every time they say the same:
I'm really needing *him*.

~

April 2000

The Bear and the Owl

The owl stays awake at night
While the bear succumbs to sleep.
The giant beast is peaceful
And knows this night the owl keeps.

The owl wants to flap his wings
And soar among the trees,
But he tries to be so quiet
So the bear won't wake and see.

The owl has things to do tonight
While the bear just wants to sleep;
If one disturbs the other,
Claws and feathers make a heap!

They each are very different—
The bear, his feathered friend.
They have a plan to get along,
A way to make amends ...

So one's awake and one's asleep,
And soon their clocks reverse.
Each one guards the other;
It's how they make it work.

~

May, 2001

Freedom

Someday, when I no longer am,
A butterfly you'll be.
I know you'll really, truly mourn,
But then you'll see you're free.

No noose too tight around your neck,
No crown of thorns to wear.
No criticisms yet to come
No arguments to bear.

Free to be or not to be,
Free to come and go.
Free to only be yourself—
And this I'll smile to know.

Many sacrifices made
And pleasures far too few.
Always doing for someone else,
But now there's time for *you*.

Be happy, oh my sweetheart,
Forgive the trying times.
And though our storms were many,
I was glad that you were mine.

Remember just the sunshine,
Forget our cloudy days.
And maybe we can play again
In that Land so far away.

So please enjoy your freedom
For I'm the one who knows
How rough you really had it—
'Tis best that first *I* go.

I love you!

~

April 2000

Our Blessing

The doctor entered, somber-faced
And said the news was bad.
She sat and tried to tell us
Just what our baby had.

It would change our lives forever,
But our baby wouldn't die.
"Just let me take my daughter home,"
Was all that I could cry.

For half a day we suffered,
Our minds a whirling mess.
And then another doctor came
Who disagreed with all the tests.

Indeed, she had been injured,
There was trauma during birth.
Within a week she would improve,
But today would be the worst.

That was fourteen years ago,
It happened like he said—
We took our little daughter home
And lay her in her bed.

She's now a graceful dancer
And her beauty grows each year.
But I never ever will forget
That day so filled with fear.

~

May 2000—For Meghan

Continued Search

He loves her in a certain way;
She loves him back the same.
But obligations aren't always pleasures,
And each plays the other's game.

Both would gladly give their lives—
That truth can't be denied.
But awkwardness is there
When they smile and utter "hi."

A deep, abiding fondness,
A happy middle ground—
I think that each is searching,
But as yet, it's not been found.

They both have built a sturdy wall
To safely hide behind.
But if these walls were tumbled
They'd like what they would find.

And so the wait continues,
As they try to find a way
To reveal to each, the other,
What forbids them so today.

~

March 2000

And So It Goes

Toddler boy meets toddler girl—
The sandbox is their toy.
They start to throw the sand around,
And each one gets annoyed.

Little boy meets little girl—
They find a swimming hole.
Right away, the splashing starts,
She pouts and tells him *no!*

Teenage boy meets teenage girl—
Things are great when first they start.
And then they think they fall in love,
Until they break each other's hearts.

Adult guy meets adult girl—
And soon the two are wed.
The honeymoon continues,
Until they bicker in their bed.

The middle age of man and woman
Can often pose a threat,
If one should start to analyze
The days since first they met.

Still later on—the Golden Years
Are quiet, more subdued.
Their fighting's done; their wars are won,
And soon they won't be two.

But while they cling and reminisce,
Still others battle on--
The War Between the Sexes
Will remain forever strong.

~

April 2001

Two

Two souls divinely united,
Two hearts happily enlightened,
Two beings are joined as one
With promises for years to come.

Young hearts are full of wonder,
While aging hearts might ponder.
Youth is a time of learning,
While later is one of yearning.

Hearts in love don't stay the same;
Time insists they have to change.
Some days they beat as only one;
Their differences are almost none.

But then they blindly turn a corner
And view the changes, since they're older.
Says the one unto the other,
"Let it be; it's not a bother."

I guess the learning never ceases
As you attempt to smooth the creases.
But truly loving, caring hearts
Commit themselves to never part.

~

May 2001

Someone Wasn't There

Everything was beautiful,
A day so planned with care.
We tried to be so happy,
But someone wasn't there.

The organ played the chorus,
And music filled the air.
People took their places,
But someone wasn't there.

Words were spoken, love exchanged;
A special time was shared.
A host of memories were made,
But someone wasn't there.

Decorations filled the rooms
With flowers everywhere.
A really festive atmosphere,
But someone wasn't there.

The band played on, and people danced;
Their love was pure and fair.
A time to be so cherished,
But someone wasn't there.

And even at the very end,
Sending off the happy pair,
Sadness filled so many
For someone wasn't there.

~

December 2000—Meghan, we missed you so much!

My Girl

My little girl is in a dorm,
Away at college, away from home,
Busily trying to pave her way
Amidst the changes of every day.

She misses us; we miss her too,
She pines for what she used to do—
The boy she had to leave behind,
The sisters who give her peace of mind.

But bravely though, her inner self
Isn't hiding upon a shelf—
She's out there fighting, marching on,
And rising up to every dawn.

She's trying unfamiliar things
And hoping every one will bring
A way to fill each empty part
That's left a void within her heart.

She met a girl who seems to care,
One who wants to talk and share.
They scout around for things to do
Always trying something new.

And so I pray that every day
She'll feel that life is more okay.
The girl who didn't think she could
Is *my girl*, and she's done it good!

~

September 2004—for Meg!

Momma

Why does Momma often cry
Alone and late at night?
She says that only she knows why
And that she'll be alright.

She says that secrets of the heart
Do sometimes stir from sleep,
And that the sadness makes her start
To feel this need to weep.

I beg her please to tell me;
I want to dry her tears.
She smiles and says to let it be,
Then draws me very near.

She holds me close and strokes my hair
And tries to wipe her eyes.
The more I tell her that I care,
The more she seems to cry.

She says someday I'll understand;
And many years from here,
I'll remember holding Momma's hand,
And things will be more clear.

They may not be the same as hers—
The tears that I will cry—
But I will know from whence they stirred,
And only I'll know why.

And it may happen late at night,
While everyone's asleep.
I'll ponder things that aren't quite right,
And I'll begin to weep.

"Go now, my sweet and darling child,"
She sends me off to bed.
I beg to stay a little while—
I know more tears are still ahead.

She smiles and says I mustn't stay;
Her thoughts will tire soon,
And back inside her heart they'll lay,
Until another late night moon.

~

November 2000—thank you, Meg.

A Very Lovely Word

I love the way they call me Momma;
The sound will never change.
A lot of things are different—
Our lives are rearranged.

But still, it doesn't matter;
It's just as sweet and pure
As once I heard so long ago
When they were children sure.

I loved their little voices;
The way they said it too.
Such a lovely, lovely word,
As sweet as morning dew.

It used to start their sentences,
And was followed by requests.
Now it comes towards the end,
When they're sending all their best.

Our lives have come full circle—
They are married, on their own.
But time can never mar
That tender word I've known!

~

April 2010

And the Two Shall Become One
—In honor of Shane and Melanie Coffey

Long ago, upon a beach,
They caught each other's eye.
He said hello, she answered back—
This youthful girl and guy.

Drawn together like a magnet
They never chose to draw apart.
Now after years of dating,
They're in each other's hearts.

They live to be together;
It doesn't matter what they do.
As long as they are partners
And do as one instead of two.

And now they're getting married,
Making plans as man and wife.
Looking for a home to share,
As they begin their married life.

So carefully, she's chosen
The gown she plans to wear,
With visions of perfection
For her groom to proudly stare.

The day is fast approaching
When she will float along the aisle
Leaning on her daddy's arm,
With a quivering little smile.

She will meet him at the altar
And there become his bride;
She will promise to be steadfast
And always at his side.

He will vow to always love her,
To be gentle and sincere.
And they will promise that together
They will see each passing year.

I hope they have a sunny day,
A harmless cloud meandering by.
And may their night be brightened with
A host of stars upon the sky.

May their wedding be as hoped for,
With every dream come true.
And may every little detail
Be magical and new.

Let love and joy surround them
With memories to share—
Enough to last a lifetime,
When this day is gone from there.

May their wedding night be blissful,
And their days thereafter calm.
And when they hold each other's hands,
Let them feel within their palms

All the love they've ever known
In all the years they've done,
And all the love they've felt, today
And in the years to come.

> God bless you,
> Momma/Lynda

~

December 30, 2000.

Anna and Dan

She loves him; he loves her back—
They're both in love and that's a fact.
Today they join as man and wife
Thus starting off a brand new life.

He's from the north, she from the south—
So this will make for quite a house.
At times the northern way will do,
And other days, they'll mix the two.

She took a while to choose her mate,
Refusing those who neared her gate.
But on an unexpected day,
She caught the glance he passed her way.

And ever since, there's only been
He for her and she for him.
They know each other's ups and downs,
When to laugh and when to frown.

Together they have journeyed far
From when she had to rent a car—
When fate stepped in and gave the nod
That now their love would come from God.

When vows are spoken, love exchanged,
She proudly takes another's name.
The rings they give they give in love
And ask for blessings from above.

Many came to share this day,
To wish them well, to join and pray
That God will let their lives be long,
And keep their marriage safe and strong.

Go forth in love as man and wife—
Rejoice in this, your married life.
May every day become more dear,
As weeks and months turn into years.

~

September 25, 2004

A Song for Meg and Garrett

Their love reads like a ballad, a sonnet, or a song—
Since first they met each other, many years have gone.
She was only but a girl, he only but a boy,
That day so long ago, when they felt that burst of joy.

He's watched her grow and blossom; he's watched her learn to dance,
And once upon a time, he earned a second chance.
They loved their way through high school, enjoyed each other's proms,
She watched him earn his money while mowing people's lawns.

They've struggled, and they've cried; they've kissed each other's tears.
They've held each other tight through one another's fears.
There's been sadness; there's been pain and times of hurt and sorrow,
But their faith has promised them a rich and strong tomorrow.

She's said she'll take his name; he's said he's glad she will—
To have his name and be his wife will make her dreams fulfilled.
To go to bed and say "goodnight" instead of saying "bye";
Just the simplicity of that is enough to make them cry.

They've learned each other's families, their moods, their ups and downs;
They know about the laughter, and here and there a frown.
They've been there for the babies and seen what that is like,
Which will help to let them know when the time for them is right.

She'll be radiant and beautiful as she slowly walks the aisle,
And their thoughts will be too many behind their nervous smiles.
They'll say the words they've dreamed about for oh–so–many years
And marvel at the wonder that their wedding's finally here.

Embarking on their honeymoon on far and distant shores,
They'll rejoice to see together things they've never seen before.
And we'll rejoice in knowing that together they are strong
And that now and in the future their love will journey on.

December 15, 2007

The Drawer

The Drawer

She had a certain, special place
She saved for only me—
Inexpensive items
She would put there lovingly.

She was kind and very thoughtful
And forever thought of me.
So when she saw a trinket,
She knew where it should be.

She didn't have to buy it—
Could be old or something new—
A pretty set of note cards
Could very easily do.

Always on the lookout
For different little whatnots—
It really seemed to please her,
These token gifts she got.

And when I came to visit,
She'd smile and say "there's more"—
So off I'd go to see
What was tucked in Mother's drawer.

~

July 2007—for love of Janice.

The Last Good-bye

They were happily trying to escape down the stairs—
A bride and her groom, as the crowd clapped and stared.
She was down in the crowd, being pushed and then shoved
In her desperate attempt to see the man she so loved.

For years, they'd been friends, best friends to each other,
Till he phoned and announced he was marrying another.
But that was okay 'cause they had never made plans,
And she had never expected a ring on her hand.

But since he had phoned her, she had suddenly known
Her friendship towards him had increasingly grown.
But too late now, for he had chosen his bride,
And she wasn't the one standing there by his side.

She choked through the wedding, walking up the long aisle;
As their maid of honor, it was her duty to smile.
Her eyes on the groom, and his back at hers,
You could tell they were thinking what used to be theirs.

With her heart nearly breaking, she forced to let go;
He gave her a nod saying yes I do know.
And then he turned, his thoughts on his bride,
And the smile on his face was a genuine sigh.

And now they were leaving, as all couples do,
The wedding festivities over and through.
The only last thing she could hope for right now
Was his glance from a distance or a wave somehow.

Too many in front of her would *not* make that so—
Sadly, she turned, getting ready to go.
It was then that she felt his hand on her shoulder—
He had come before leaving to hug and to hold her.

He deeply looked on her tearful face,
Such warmth and sadness in their last embrace.
He lovingly smiled and then whispered bye,
She did the same and tried not to cry.

He had given to her, her final wish,
Before he embarked on his wedded bliss.
He had taken a wife and married her then,
But he'd never forget his very best friend!

~

November 2003—after the film *My Best Friend's Wedding*

The Dance

The lights were bright, the room aglow,
She wanted so to dance.
The band played every song she knew—
Still, she didn't have a chance.
Her girlfriend said that she should come
If only just this time,
But this was such a bad mistake—
And now a ride she'd have to find.
Then suddenly before her
Stood a giant of a man—
Amazed at what he asked her,
She reached up and took his hand.
He waltzed her round the ballroom floor;
His grip was firm and tight.
Now she knew why Cinderella
Could have danced all night.
Too soon, the dance was over
But he was asking for another—
As he placed her in her wheelchair,
She said he needn't bother.
He vowed the pleasure would be his
And would she kindly not refuse?
So once again, he carried her,
And ever since, he's been her shoes.

~

April 2000

Pioneer Night

The winter night grew colder still,
She poked the fire to ease the chill.
The children were sleeping, tucked in their beds—
Too young to know of the cold night ahead.

They were covered in quilts her mother had made,
A gift to be cherished and always be saved.
She thought of her mom, who had begged them to stay
As they left for the prairies that long ago day.

They had wanted the freedom to be one with the land,
To raise their own crops, to toil with their hands.
They left in a wagon, three children in tow,
To a part of the country they were yearning to know.

They had built their wood cabin, small but secure
Enough to withstand the harsh winters out here.
But this was their first and harder, they feared,
Than what they'd expected when coming out here.

Late summer and autumn had been good to them all;
The children had played in the animal stalls.
The barn they built housed a horse and a cow—
She was hoping that both were warm enough now.

The horse had been used in the field that they plowed
Their crop had been small, but they managed somehow.
The children were young but had learned to do chores
And were anxiously waiting to play in the snow.

The winter had come—the snow and the wind.
Their cabin stood fearless again and again.
Tonight, she was worried—the blizzard was strong—
Seemed hours ago her husband had gone.

It was light when he left, but now it was dark,
He was checking the barn, the wood, the livestock.
She sat by the fire and started her knitting,
All the while worrying, wondering, listening.

Suddenly, the wind blew open the door!
Covered in snow, he had made it once more.
Enough wood for the fire and love for his wife,
They nestled together for a pioneer night.

~

December 2004

And Now a Little Boy

They've just found out about their son—
They're going to have a boy.
And all of us they've told
Are overcome with joy.

A new tradition has begun
In a family blessed with girls.
For now, we'll have a little son
To complete our little world.

It wasn't any accident—
Indeed 'twas very planned—
First God and then my mom
Worked together hand in hand.

The very night my mother died
I gave her this request:
"My daughter needs a baby,
Please, Momma, do your best."

She took me very seriously—
It was high upon her list—
Not long was she in heaven
Before my daughter got her wish.

For years, she felt such panic
That perhaps she'd not conceive—
So when Momma spoke to God,
She knew how great the need.

She helped Him make his tiny wings—
She helped to make them strong.
When God and Mom were finished,
God gently sent him on.

A little boy or little girl—
So long before we knew.
But his baby cousin, Kaylee,
Knew we'd buy him blue.

She'd pat my daughter's tummy
Then tilt her face to see
The mother of the babe she's known
For all eternity.

I know they speak the language
The angels taught them to—
And once they played in heaven
Like unborn babies do.

She'll welcome him the day he's born,
He'll smile to see her face.
And she can reassure him
He'll love his little place.

She'll teach him all the how-to's
She's learned in just a year—
How great to have a mom and dad
To love you when you're here.

Again, they'll play together,
And romp around this world—
Again to love each other,
This little boy and girl.

~

December 2006—for love of Jackson and Kaylee and … thank–you,
Momma!

A Place of Many Miracles

There's a special place for preemies,
For tiny, little newborns—
A place where angel-nurses
Strive to keep them safe and warm.
The room is large; the lights are dimmed,
And incubator beds
Are homes for precious beings
Who were born a bit ahead.
It's a place where modern science
And God together heal,
Where hopes and dreams and prayers
And miracles are real.
So helpless as they struggle
These tiny boys and girls—
Too long before they're ready
To live within our world.
How skilled these angel-nurses,
How compassionate and kind
As they toil to save these babies
Each moment at a time.
Thank-you, God, for such a place,
For the knowledge and the care,
And the hopeful gift of knowing
That You, Yourself, are there.

~

April 2007

A Grandmother's Prayer

My mother never told me
This thought that Grandma's fear:
We have to answer to our children
When their little ones are here.
The thought of something happening
To a child when in my care—
Even if it weren't my fault
Leaves me horrified and scared.
These little ones are really fast
And stronger than you'd think.
A minute can be way too long;
It can happen in a blink.
I left my children with my mom
A thousand different times,
But never did she mention
A dreaded fear like mine.
I'd love to have a dozen
Of these precious little souls,
For every small and priceless one
Will steal my heart I know.
Maybe they will teach me
If I do the best I can
And pray to God for blessings,
They'll be safe when in my hands.

~

March 2008

My Greatest Honor

My grandson laughed today.
His laugh was just for me—
He thinks it's just the greatest
To play peek-a-boo with me.

A few short minutes later,
My granddaughter so happily
Squeals "Ma'maw, come let's play—
We'll pretend we're having tea!"

This joyous sound of voices,
So small and ever sweet—
Their busy little bodies
And swiftly moving feet.

What did we do without them?
I can't remember what—
They've so enriched our lives,
Their play so fun to watch.

Their smiles are like the sunshine,
They warm me with delight—
Their gorgeous, glistening eyes
As bright as stars at night.

To hear them whisper, "Please don't go,"
Is such a compliment.
It makes me feel I did okay,
This time together spent.

They honor me with love
Beyond my greatest dream.
I praise You for these two
And those I've yet to see.

~

March 2008—for love of my grandchildren, now and in the future.

Life Allowed an Answer

That silent love she nurtured
So long ago in youth
Has spoken back to her
With loving words of truth.

Nevermore the teens
Who shared a day back then—
They only spoke with innocence
And words they truly meant.

They knew what they were feeling,
But life had things to say—
At the end of every summer
She was made to go her way.

Now they write to one another,
Exploring niceties—
That works a while, but then you're bored
And wanting life to tell you more.

And so we have—we've taken risks
With secrets we have shared,
But never stepping out of bounds
On those we love and care.

The clocks for us are older,
But both of us have tried
To be so ever grateful—
Life answered, by-and-by.

~

April 2010—for love of Gary

III

A Lantern on
Faith, God, and His Creations

I Ask of Thee

Oh God of wisdom, God of words,
Let my prayer tonight be heard.

On my knees, all noise away,
I'll close my eyes and start to pray.

Bless the peoples of this land,
Spread over us Thy Mighty Hand.

Relieve the pain from all the ill,
And give to them Your Own Goodwill.

Remember those who live in fear
Of what might come to them this year.

Bless my home so it can be
A safe place for my family.

Help us all, so we'll be strong,
That we might know the right from wrong.

Guide us through our work, our play,
Take our troubles from each day.

Help our lands to find a peace
That all our wars might finally cease.

Oh God of all, please hear my plea
Consider these requests for me.
      Amen

~

Early 1960s

God Is Near

God is like a guide to you—
He watches o'er and helps us too.
He helps us in our work and play,
In every little thing each day,
  God is near.

In every week,
In every day,
In every moment that I pray,
  God is near.

God is in both you and me—
God is there in all we see.
In every step I try to walk
In every word I try to talk,
  God is near.

When trouble stirs the air
You can't see Him, but He's there.
He'll save you from all harm—
So do not be alarmed.
  God is near.

Now I've told what God can do—
How He can be a friend to you.
Now it's time for you to give
Your heart to Him in which He'll live.
  God is near.

~

Mid 1960s

Walk in the Meadow

It was still quite early in the morn,
Although the sun had just been born.
Upon the earth, it spread its rays
To make this bright, warm, sunny day.

Over the meadow, I thought I'd roam
To hear the crickets in their homes.
And then to look around and see
Other things that interest me.

The grass was cut so short and green,
A little bug crawling could easily be seen.
The flowers looked so bright and gay,
Moved by the wind in a gentle sway.

The trees in the distance—green and tall—
Made me look so short and small.
I love to walk the meadows free—
Just Mother Nature and happy me.

~

Early 1960s, when I was very young. I first fell in love with a meadow
on my aunt's farm.

Little Spider

Little spider on the wall—
Where is it that you want to crawl?
You seem to live without a goal
Retracing all your steps of old.

Just where did you originate?
You're just a small thing, born of late.
I wonder where might be the nest
From which you've wondered from the rest.

For three days now, you've lived alone—
That vacant wall has been your home.
You do not eat, but yet survive,
And still you try to stay alive.

I wonder what will be your death—
When will you take your final breath?
Perhaps there is a preplanned fate
For this little spider, born of late.

Compared to life you matter not,
No more than just a tiny dot.
And yet you're big enough alone
To be the center of my poem.

~

Mid 1960s when I was sick in bed with the flu as a child, watching a
spider on my wall.

St. Mary's Street

The old proud trees are wise and good
While standing tall, as time knew they would.
Their great wide branches bend to meet
To form an arc above
      St. Mary's Street.

One can hear them whispering low
Late at night when no one goes.
In the day, they smile back down to greet
The passersby on
      St. Mary's Street.

These stately creatures towering high
Enjoy the wind on her journey by.
And to shelter those from the summer's heat
They provide the shade on
      St. Mary's Street.

Their leaves are a deep refreshing green,
With the glimmer of sunlight in between.
These majestic trees, so prim and neat,
Are a lovely view on
      St. Mary's Street.

They've long been standing tall and fine,
Having seen and accepted the changes of time.
They've weathered the storms without defeat,
And they're proud to stand on
      St. Mary's Street.

They add some beauty to every day
With their towering strength and gentle sway.
And with those in the past, I'll again repeat:
God Bless the trees on
      St. Mary's Street.

~

Early 1970s

The Rain

The rain is coming down in sheets;
The world is dull and gray.
Upon the helpless trees it beats
And fallen leaves are blown away.

The sky is dark; the sun has gone.
In silence all are lying
In wait to see what lies beyond
The sound of nature's crying.

~

Early 1970s

The Midnight Sea

The day has finally closed its doors;
The sun has shut her eyes.
Above the far and distant shores,
Prevail the darkening skies.

The sea—so calm and full of grace,
A picture of repose.
And yet her waters never cease
To capture friend or foe.

Her form, so harmless in the day,
She welcomes all in sight.
Alas—but now you'll be her prey,
If encountered in the night.

Her waves are stronger—deep and dark—
They roar as in rejoice,
For now the bravest of the larks
Flies not above her frightening voice.

At times, so rich in awe and grace,
A lady she can be—
Until the time she changes face,
To become the midnight sea.

~

Fall 1979

Divinely Painted Picture

Blue-gray mountains, silver streams
Grassy meadows, these, my dreams.

So majestic are my hills
Silhouetted and so still.

Oh, the meadows, luscious green
Cattle grazing, quiet scene.

Wish I could with brush in hand
Paint the mountains of this land.

To paint like God would be divine
I paint with words, each stroke, a line.

I look upon the valleys low
And into them I long to go.

Each time I come from where I've been
My soul proclaims I'm home again.

I'd like to ask that when I die
Beneath these hills, please, let me lie.

~

May 1984

Nature's Dominion

The wildness of the weather
Dost wake my soul from slumber,
And I feel my spirit soaring
At the awesome crackling thunder.
An angry, darkened sky
Like a woman close to birth—
Its bulging, heaving clouds
In a fury soon to burst.
Great waterfalls of rain
Driven hard by gusts of wind,
And crystal balls of hail
Mimic that of falling tin.
Like the fireworks of summer
That illuminate the sky,
So the lightning round me flashes,
Too blinding for the eye.
How magnificent the wind
Exhibiting such power.
And bow do I to Mother Nature
Who took command and spoke this hour.
Mortal man is thus reminded
However vast his knowledge be—
God hath given timeless Nature
Dominion over thee.

~

January 1989

Sky Before Storm

Stark and dark ... foreboding.
Vivid and violet ... awesome.
Turning, churning ... and changing
Rapidly moving ... tumultuous.
Wild and windy ... wondrous.
Bold and beautiful ... beckoning.
Mother Nature ... exquisite painter
Obeying ... her Master's sigh:
Paint a storm ... across my sky.

And afterwards ... the rain.
Darkened sky ... sadly tamed.
A rainbow there ... certain proof,
The sky reborn ... gone the storm.

~

August 1987

Winter

It's winter:
Cold ... and ... gray ... and ... bare
Halloween's gone, and so is the fair.
Christmas:
A couple of weeks away—
(I wish that Santa Claus could stay.)

What to do ... in January?
What to do ... when I'm contrary?
Winter:
It's cold and gray and bare—
At naked trees, I'm forced to stare.
Summer grass—
Dead and gone.
I grieve for freshly new-mown lawns.
Autumn leaves—
Rotting brown
Staying where they fall, I frown.
Winter:
Cold and dull and gray—
Red birds all have flown away.

Rigid schedules to abide—
Kids to school in carpool rides.
Reading, math, projects too—
Always something else to do.

It's winter:
Dull and bare and cold.
I'm up before the sun takes hold.
The house
So chilled and still asleep
I barely stumble to my feet.

Winter evenings:
Dark and gray—
Children early in from play.
Days are short, but chores are long—
When next you look, the day is gone.

Winter months:
Drag on and on
March—
Has even yet to come.
When it does, my soul will soar ...
There's April—
Tugging winter's door!

Sweet April
And her sister May—
Holding hands
They shyly say,
"Die down winter, don't you know—
The time has come for you to go."

Oh, winter:
Dark and dull and gray
Still you linger on each day.
And so my spirit sadly waits
To bloom in spring when winter breaks.

~

December 1982—I felt this way about the winter before I moved to our mountains and the snow.

His Majesty In The Mountains

'Twas told to me not long ago
That in a garden, fair,
You'd surely find the Heart of God
If you'd but tarry there …

That all throughout the Bible
Many gardens do abound,
And in among the flowers,
God's Spirit can be found.

I do not doubt that this be true.
For yes, indeed I know
God truly loves a garden
As the Scriptures clearly show.

But, I too, know a special place
I feel our God to be:
For high upon the mountaintops
Dwells He, majestically.

'Tis in among the lilies
One sees His gentler side,
But deep within the mountains
The strength of God abides.

And in the gardens many,
His compassion can be found;
For amidst His blooming tulips,
He never wears His frown.

But on the rolling hillsides,
The meadows green and still,
Among the cattle grazing there
The peace of God prevails.

And so, for some it may be true—
Within a garden's walls,
Among the perfumed blossoms there,
You hear Him gently call.

Not so for me. I see His face
Upon a mountain's wall.
And in the valleys stretched below
I see Him there the best of all.

~

March, 1984

Home from the Mountains

I read a poem 'long time ago
'Bout a "mariner home from the sea."
I wonder now was he as sad
As I, when home from where I long to be?

But it is not the ocean
That can bring my heart to grieve—
Instead these Blue Ridge Mountains
Are what I hate to leave.

Such sadness comes upon me
Each time I go away.
And to this heavy heart, I vow
That soon I'll come to stay.

~

October 1985

Hills of Healing

Hills of Healing

Stretching out before her
The quiet mountains stood.
Strong, yet never moving
As only mountains could.
She parked her car and locked the doors
And settled down to watch
> The dusk that soon would settle
> Upon this silent, hilly notch.

Troubled when she first arrived
They've calmed and soothed her soul
These old and rugged mountains
Can make a spirit whole.
Their message never changes
They always seem to say
> Come hither unto us and pause
> We'll ease your cares away.

As if patiently awaiting
And knowing she would come
They quickly work their magic
And in little time, they're done.
She breathes a sigh and whispers thanks
And starts her car to leave
> The mountains know she'll come again
> To seek their strength and peace.

~

April 1994

A Field of Daisies

I saw a field of daisies
Swaying in the breeze
Appearing unattended.
May I wander through it please?

My question drew no answer
For no one was around.
Who owns a field of daisies
This far away from town?

There isn't any farm nearby
No homestead I can see.
How came this field of daisies
That is calling out to me?

I seem to sense a loneliness
I think it needs a friend.
I promise, field of daisies
That I will come again.

If no one else will claim you
I'll take you as my own.
Fear not, my field of daisies
No more you'll be unknown.

~

January 1988

Softly Summer

The rain beyond my window
So gently does it fall
Amidst the blend of sultry air
'Tis hardly heard at all.

How sweet the smell of springtime
Its warm and gentle breeze
So welcomed from the arctic winds.
Mourns not that winter leaves.

Life is recreated
All nature born anew
Its silent hibernations
Burst forth amid the dew.

Steadily and quietly
Awakening from its slumber
Gently nudging winter on
Softly comes the summer.

~

February 1988

First Snowfall

Such a winter wonderland
A world made white with snow.
All of God's Creation
Transformed within its glow.

The hush and stillness in the air
Can creep within your soul.
The peace that comes with such a calm
Not often do we know.

The ever falling stars of snow
Noses pressed against the pane.
Excited children beg to know
How much snow is in the lane.

And such a change it is to see
These woods so dressed in white
Like a thousand lighted candles
Burning strong throughout this night.

Thus quietly a hopefulness
Is born within my self:
Perhaps the good and beautiful
Can win above all else.

~

February 1989

Darkest Night

No moon or stars, no nighttime light—
Thus shadows dance with great delight.
Beyond my left, beyond my right
I only see this darkest night.
Total blackness everywhere—
I think the trees are even scared!

I wonder—will there come the dawn
Or must this night stretch ever on,
Where the lights that hours past
Allowed us hope the day would last?

So different be this night from day—
One guides, the other hides our way.
One beckons *come,* the other calls
Better not proceed at all!
Friendly day, though, sees our flaws,
While blackened night erases all.
And those of nature's peaceful scenes:
Mountains, meadows, fishing streams,
So vivid all throughout the day,
Are found at night to back away.

I know that night must follow day
For long ago 'twas planned that way.
And know I do we need the rest,
Each creature in its given nest.
And yes, the dawn will surely come
When night so signals it is done.

But it is comforting to me
If through this blackness I can see
A ray of light that softly calls,
The darkness didn't conquer all!

~

October 1985

Song of the Wind Chimes

Song of the Wind Chimes

The wind sails across my window
The wind chimes ring their song
And for just so brief a moment
On the wind, I ride along.

I leave the busy city
And journey far from home
To a land beyond the ocean
Indeed, 'tis not my own.

The gentle sound of wind chimes
Reminds my weary self
Of quiet, rolling hillsides
And the shepherd's simple wealth.

The blue and spacious skies
The meadow he calls home
The echoing of sheep bells
Are what he truly owns.

The busy chirping crickets
The whispering of the wind
The playful mountain sheep
Become his quiet friends.

Serene and quite unhurried
He breathes the mountain air.
Does he know beyond his hillside
Another world lives there?

My wind chime's fallen silent
Likewise, the wind is still.
And home again am I
From the shepherd's lonely hill.

~

April 1988

Letter to God

I need to know the reasons
For these sad and senseless things.
I need my questions answered—
I need life to lose its sting.

There's grief at every corner;
It never seems to end.
You hear of someone's sorrow …
Then you hear it struck again.

Too sad to even comprehend
The fate that some must bear.
Such grief, it pierces through the heart:
Oh, God, are still You there?

So oft' it's You who stand aside
Allowing things to be;
Regardless of our pain and hurt,
Do not You care to see?

I know You, too, have suffered
When You sacrificed Your Son—
But that meant He rose to meet You,
And then Your grief was done.

But here it seems so different
Cause when those we love ascend,
Our grief is not then conquered:
Instead, it just begins.

We're left alone and empty
When those we love depart.
Our days don't seem to matter;
We're left an aching heart.

For some, a long and lingering death—
We watch through painful eyes.
And yet again, some others
Are called to quickly die.

Surely, You must see our pain
When You quickly take away.
Here this minute, gone the next,
Sudden grief in just a day.

So life is far too fragile;
It makes one wonder why
If life can be so snatched away,
What good to even try?

Oh, yes, there *is* a Heaven,
Of this, I fully trust.
And only You, God, with Your Son,
Will give Eternity to us.

It isn't this I question,
It isn't this I doubt.
I simply want to understand
What *this* life is all about.

So oft' it seems You pick and choose
At random who You call,
Regardless of our earnest prayers
We prayed *so* hard for *all.*

And thus, I often wonder
About this thing called prayer—
Is there really power in it?
Does it change Your mind up there?

Do you come to a decision
On the prayers that You're receiving?
Or do You carry out Your will
Regardless of our pleading?

I've come to feel the latter—
That yes, You want our prayers,
But mainly to acknowledge
That we *do* believe You're there.

That You chose this way for us
To express to You our views,
To tell You what we really hope
That in the end You'll do.

But knowing in that final end
No matter what we pray,
Because You *are* the Master—
You will choose to have Your way.

I've read the Bible almost through—
The Scriptures one by one:
Believe in what you pray for
As if it were thus done.

But that is then presuming
That *we* will have our way.
Then another verse does tell us,
In the end, God has *His* say.

So our prayers express opinions,
Though we know You have the power
To change the course of all events
Regardless of the hour.

Not necessarily will You choose
To do what we have prayed—
For if it doesn't fit Your plan
Our wishes then are stayed.

The many Scriptures do imply
Our only goal should be
To set our sights for Heaven's door,
To seek Eternity.

And this I want for those I love,
I want it, too, for me,
Dear Lord, but in the meantime
I ache at what I see.

The tragic things that happen
While we strive to join You there—
The awful pain we suffer—
It seems to me unfair.

Each sorrow makes me question,
Though I know it's not my place,
You could have interceded
With Your instant saving Grace.

But yet You chose to step aside
To satisfy Your will.
And this is what I agonize:
At times, You seem too still.

Your ways should not be questioned—
The Bible makes this clear.
But just some simple answers
Would make it better here.

If no, You cannot give them,
Would You consider, please,
To intervene a little more
On all these tragedies?

Or maybe You can show us
New ways that we can cope—
What thoughts to think to reassure,
Despite our grief, there's hope.

I've written here my views, Dear God,
This, then, I'll call a prayer.
And know I do, You'll read it
When it's handed to You there.

~

November 1987

Why

He died ...
Just eight months old
My being aches
It wants to know
The reasons why
To make some sense
To justify
The pain we bear
Our minds are tense
Can doubt we dare?
Might numbness be
From day to day
A way to cope
Put doubt away?
But numbness pales
Then what remains
A bleeding heart
That can't refrain
It pleads again
Oh why?
Faith unknowing
Believing unseen.
Though blind keep going
His love redeems
Yea, we are taught
So we should learn
A baby died
Questions still burn
No answers come
I've asked in vain
There's but one choice
Go forth in pain
Believing yes
Believing no
The choice is ours
The search is slow

Onward journey
Believe will I
Yet still my soul
Will cry out *Why?*

~

February 1989—for love of Brian

First Painful Year

Today is spent in anguish.
'Tis now a year ago
He reluctantly departed
To that place we little know.

A calendar of painful times,
Occasions come and gone.
And every one was further proof
His absence made it wrong.

This month will mark a final end
To a year so wrought with *firsts*.
Such days and nights of agony,
Yet *his* soul has known rebirth.

The loneliness continues.
For some, it ceases not.
The image of his earthliness
Not soon to be forgot.

I know what he would say
If the chance were given him …
Words of comfort he would speak
To those whose hearts are dim:

> Remember me, but smiling
> (I can hear his pleading tone).
> I have simply changed locations
> And moved away, back Home.

> My life was good, without regrets,
> 'Tis even better here!
> Please believe this simple truth:
> I await you all my dears.

Can time permit acceptance
To permeate the mind
And allow the grieving heart
Contentment it might find?

Perhaps this second year ahead,
Though our aching cannot cease,
Will alleviate our pain enough
To find an inner peace.

~

June 1989—for love of Roy

The Architects

The architect was brilliant;
His design a masterpiece—
Complete with stained glass windows,
Considered quite a feat.

Its pillars made of marble,
And rooms adorned with gold,
Exquisite, modern hallways
Invited young and old.

Towering high among the trees,
Silhouetted o'er the town,
A landmark for its people
And viewed for miles around.

Many hours far from here
Beyond this concrete maze,
Another busy architect
Constructs with little praise.

His buildings are the mountains
Rising tall and just as strong.
They too are silhouetted
On the clouds that journey on.

The rooms, replaced by meadows,
No hallways, only trails.
The roof, an endless skyline
Allowing wind the space to sail.

Void of stained glass windows,
This builder chose to use
The brilliance of a sunset
Ablaze with vivid hues.

Two architects among us,
Each has given of himself.
We hold our own opinions
Which art holds greater wealth.

The tragedy I offer,
The wrong we should not trod,
Occurs when handiworks of man
Invade the art of God.

~

May 1990

The Rainbow

High upon a mountaintop
I thought I heard my God.
And in the swaying trees
I was sure I saw Him nod.

The eerie, silent solitude
Gave way for Him to speak,
And on the wind, I heard His Voice—
'Twas gentle, low, and meek.

How great the thrill to hear Him
Where most I love to be—
High upon that mountain
He chose to speak to me!

And so I vowed to always stay—
A fool to leave such ground.
But thus, He then commanded
I should go and journey down.

I pleaded so on bended knees:
If I do leave from here,
Perhaps I'll lose this moment
That now I hold so dear.

With understanding gentleness,
He knew this time would fade,
So promised He would send a sign
That He alone had made:

To drive away your grief and doubt
And be assured 'tis true
That yes, indeed, we've had this time,
These moments swift and few,

Look high toward my Heaven
And I will prove to thee
That I have not forgotten
This day you've had with Me.

Despairingly, I left Him,
A grief I'd never known.
So sure was I such happiness
Again I'd never own.

Later, down the mountain
Amidst a busy street,
Pretending to be happy
To those I had to greet,

A sudden warmth did fill the air
And color streaked the sky;
Mine eyes were lifted upward
And to my great surprise,

There, arched toward His Heaven,
A rainbow stretched for miles:
My God had kept His promise
And my heart could see Him smile.

February 1990

The Storm and Me

The howling wind, the driving rain,
Such wild and wicked weather.
A sky of lightning, crackling thunder,
The noisier, the better.
Wonder why, I feel this thrill to
See such storms amidst—
But I do know my saddened soul,
When long they go amiss.

An angry sky, a darkened hour, the
Bright of day retreats,
And once again, a threatening storm
Commands to those it meets.
Perhaps the risk of danger, the need
Of shelter for a while;
And interruptions of the moment
Give cause for me to smile.

When next a storm approaches,
This quirk of mine within
Prepares itself to savor nature's fury,
Yet again.
Exhilarated feelings, short lived,
They didn't last,
Another storm, too quickly, once more
Becomes the past.

~

May 1990

Passing Leaves

The dancing leaves of autumn
Cascading deftly down—
Their gentle rustling forms a song,
Chanting forth the autumn sounds.

The naked trees from whence they came
Are sad to see them go.
For know, they do, it won't be long
Until their branches hang with snow.

And then their friends, the fallen leaves,
Buried deep beneath the cold—
Their gold and crimson colors
Gone brown and stale and old.

But past the winter, blooms the spring,
Creating life anew.
And once again within the trees,
Infant buds are wet with dew.

Instead of barren branches,
The trees now cloaked in green,
Emerging forth from tiny sprouts,
The leaves are being weaned.

This miracle of cycles
Nears completion once again,
As nature now replaces
Those autumn leaves back then.

~

March 1993

Autumn Days

When there's dew atop the pumpkin
And frost upon the ground,
When summer leaves turn crimson,
Then fall has settled down.

The leaves too quickly tumble,
Replacing summer's rain.
They sadly leave their lovely trees
Barren once again.

The cold and crispy mornings,
A sweater donned at dusk,
A darkened sky at early hour,
And shorter days for us.

When children start to worry
Which costume will suffice,
A princess or a pirate,
Then Halloween is close in sight.

The ripened crops are harvested
As fields are swiftly plowed—
Since nature plans to hibernate,
There's little time allowed.

Such grandeur in these mountains,
Bright oranges, reds, and golds—
One can only stand in awe
Of what autumn has bestowed.

As winter fast approaches
With its promises of snow,
Wise is he who steadfast holds
To this splendor 'fore it goes.

~

October 1993

Almost Snow

A thousand flakes are drifting
Like tons of tumbling stars,
And by their windows watching,
My children gasp in awe.

This long-awaited snowfall,
The first this season brings—
Our mountain town falls silent,
Prepared for winter's sting.

The howling wind, like roaring trains,
Pierces through the night;
Exhausted trees, though swayed, still stand,
Undaunted by its fierce delight.

Sadly though, the snow is blown
Across our fields and farms,
Permitted not to paint a scene
Of wintry snowy charm.

And thus, the storm blows yonder,
And with it grimly goes
Our great anticipation
Of a carnival of snow.

Reluctantly, my children
Succumb and drag to bed,
But only with the constant hope
Swirling through their heads

That surely there is yet the day
When snow will swiftly fall,
Draping white our homes and barns
Like newly knitted shawls.

When snowmen stand erected,
And sleds break record speeds,
'Tis then our mountain town will boast
We got the snow we need!

~

January 1992

Winter White

The trees outside my window
Tonight are proud to know
That their magnificent Creator
Has covered them with snow.

The snow fell down without the wind,
And so the woods were still.
And every flake that entered them
Stayed quiet till the trees were filled.

From early on, such changes—
Their branches dark as night.
But now their arms unfolded
Show their limbs so gloved in white.

Such a perfect, painted picture,
A contrast undenied—
From barren trees to wedding white,
The envy of my eyes.

What a splendid plan prepared
To have these trees in summer
Dressed in leaves to shade and shelter
Till the winter when they slumber.

And just when all their beauty's lost,
With nothing fine for them to show,
There comes a day that lifts our hearts—
Naked trees all decked in snow!

~

February 1999

Snowy Hour

I will always well remember
When in my kitchen dark
I sat alone one evening late
To stare at trees with snowy bark.

For just beyond my window
Was a vast array of white—
The trees so laden down with snow
Filled the dark with light.

From early dusk to later hour
They captured so my thoughts
And filled my head with visions
Of the peacefulness they brought.

I wrote it down on paper—
This night of snowy trees—
Reflecting on how special
Their beauty meant to me.

~

February 1999

The Blizzard

Beyond my door, the blizzard rages;
The piercing wind forever shifts.
Our fields and lanes are camouflaged
'Neath walls of snowy drifts.

The woods that once were littered
With a potpourri of flaws,
Are magically converted
To a winterland of awe.

The trees have donned their winter coats,
Their limbs are gloved in white.
The creeks are capped with settled snow,
While fences fade from sight.

Our town is quickly silenced
As the blizzard pushes on.
Stranded people homeward bound—
For some, this day is long.

A time for older children
To test the speed of sleds.
While younger ones are begging
For the *man of snow* instead.

And so the blizzard rages,
And thrilled am I again
To be a part of such a storm
And sad for when it ends.

~

March 1993

The Deer within the Woods

The Deer within the Woods

Appearing very suddenly,
Emerging from our woods,
Tall and ever-cautious,
The deer so stately stood.

Alert to every passing sound,
Prepared to turn in flight,
Such gracefulness of movement,
These creatures quick and light.

Protective of each other,
They graze a chosen spot.
Always peering round about,
Afraid of being caught.

Never meaning any harm
They seek a sheltered place—
The quiet woods to raise their young,
Retreating there in haste.

Too often falling victim—
The hunter's chosen prey—
Alarmed by sudden movement,
They turn to dart away.

The silence rudely shattered,
A helpless buck goes down.
These woods he thought were tranquil
Became a hunting ground.

So goes the plight of many deer,
An undeserving fate.
Come, dwell in peace you gentle ones—
Upon my land, you're safe.

February 1994

Shadows of the Woods

These woods at night lie deep and dark,
The scent of pine and touch of bark,
Not quite as obvious as when
The light of day starts peeking in.

Shadows cast their eerie forms,
While dancing through the branches torn.
Accompanied by whistling wind,
They dance until the dawn begins.

There, watching from a nearby limb,
The owl sternly studies them.
Unaware that also he
Another nightly shadow be.

And scampering through these darkened woods,
Instead of sleeping as they should,
The cottontails are playing chase,
Pursued by squirrels with equal haste.

The owl screeches forth disgust,
Annoyed at all this silly fuss.
He views these woods at night as his,
Thus closely eyeing all that is.

And peeping out from round a tree,
Whose slanted yellow eyes are these?
Another shadow slides away,
A nightly creature out for prey.

And thus, these woods are silent not,
Engrossed, instead, with sounds that wrought
A certain fear to him who dares
Invade this dark and wooded lair.

~

March 1992

Mountain Missing

I left the hills for just a day
To go and visit friends.
But in that shortened time away,
My thoughts returned again.

I missed the grassy meadow beds,
The lazy, grazing cows.
And round each curve and just ahead,
A mountain's stately prow.

I missed three crosses on a hill
That rise above the town—
The way they stand so straight and still,
Though guarding those around.

I missed the stillness in the air
That comes with early morn,
The patchy fog that settles there,
Before the day is worn.

I missed the echo of the crow,
Its eerie, chilling call.
Its graceful flight to where it goes,
This blackest bird of all.

I missed the quiet, country lanes
That slowly snake along,
The whistle of a mountain train,
The creekbed's babbling song.

And so my thoughts retreated back
Away from city sights.
I knew that I could only stay
But just a couple nights.

The mountains, meadows, country roads
Would lure me hither there,
Entreating me to linger long—
Thus echoing my silent prayer.

~

November 1991

The Incomprehensible

Who can ever comprehend
The rugged canyon walls—
Its soaring depths, its magnitude,
Its silent, beckoning call?

Who can ever comprehend
Its vast and open space?
It paralyzes so the mind,
Rejecting one's embrace.

Who can ever comprehend
The way it all began …
One wild and racing river
Carving history through the land?

Who can ever comprehend
What spans six billion years …
The plight of ancient peoples
Who lived and journeyed here?

Who can ever comprehend
Its grandeur and its grace,
From breathless views upon its rim
To rushing rapids at its base?

Who can ever comprehend
Its eerie solitude;
So hushed within its vastness—
To speak seems almost rude.

Who can ever comprehend
The strength and quiet peace
It offers forth without an end—
Who could ever comprehend?
Not I.

~

July 1990

So Where Was God Today?

A woman dies with unborn twins—
A freakish thing they say—
Her idling car ran over her.
So where was God today?

A policeman shot while helping out—
The car just sped away—
Someone's husband, someone's dad.
So where was God today?

Nearby, within a children's ward,
Two parents kneel to pray—
Their helpless child is dying.
Will God be there today?

A house has burned beyond control—
Three sleeping children lay—
Family members weeping.
Where on earth was God today?

A drunken driver falls asleep—
He's not the one who pays—
A husband, wife, and children.
So where was God today?

A man is masked and robs a store—
Each shopper told to stay—
One by one, he kills them all.
Was God around today?

A woman drowns her toddlers—
She cries and looks away.
Why couldn't God have stopped her?
Where was God that day?

A plane goes down with all on board—
So many so afraid—
Helpless but to sit and wait.
Please, where was God this day?

More questions go unanswered.
Yet only One can say
That yes, He does remember
Just where He was that day.

~

February 1998

A Quiet Place to Go

The sea is calm; the moon is full,
Casting light upon the shore.
A thousand people from the day
Will soon be back for more.

But as for now, the beach is hers;
She sees herself alone.
She finds a roll of tumbleweed,
And tonight she'll call it home.

Close by, there lies some driftwood;
She will set it by the weeds,
And cuddling with a blanket,
Is all that she will need.

Perfect peace and solitude,
No worries, pain, or sorrow.
Just the wonderment of nature,
Without a thought about tomorrow.

She'll watch the ocean's rise and fall,
The breaking of the foam.
With no one near to interrupt,
She can call the sea her own.

The night is not completely dark;
The moon becomes her friend.
She isn't scared to be alone
And hates to see it end.

A balmy breeze blows 'cross her hair;
The taste of salt is strong.
The ocean's scent is soothing,
Like an old familiar song.

She mustn't sleep; she stays awake
To savor every hour.
Her heart and mind are opened wide
To feel the ocean's power.

But as the dawn approaches,
She will gather up her things
And leave the spot that gave her strength
To face the day and what it brings.

~

2001—for love of Janice

Another Place To Go
   —For me

Let me find a little cabin
Where no one ever goes,
With distant snowcapped mountains
And a quiet lake below.

Perfect peace and solitude
No worries, pain, or sorrow.
Just the wonderment of nature,
Without a thought about tomorrow.

A raging rain has churned the lake,
The sky's ablaze with lightening.
The pounding of the thunder—
An excited sense of frightening.

Soon a crispness fills the air;
The autumn trees are shifting.
The lake is filled with color,
As the leaves are gently drifting.

Then the greatest wonder ever ...
A gentle snow-filled night.
Snowflakes large and silent
Falling everywhere in sight.

They settle on my doorstep;
They hug my windowpane.
I feel the cold upon my face—
For now, my world is sane.

And in the snow, a darkened form—
The gentle creature fears—
He's learned I'd never hurt him,
So reluctantly, he nears.

So still am I, to lure him on,
He hesitates but comes—
Until a sound so scares him off,
The deer and I were one.

Back inside, a fire warms
My humble, safe abode.
Let me stay forever here
And happily grow old.

~

September 2001

Sounds

Can you hear the solitude
High within these hills?
Alone and one with nature,
With everything so still?
      I can.

Do you hear the blackbird
Close by within that tree?
Do you think his constant cawing
Is directed just at me?
      I do.

Do you hear the mooing cows
Not so far away?
Grazing on the ridges
Late this summer's day?
      I can.

A very high and distant plane,
Too high to see, for sure.
Do you wonder where it's going?
Does the pilot know he's heard?
      I wonder.

Chirping birds within the woods
Singing all day long.
Such tiny little creatures
And a hundred different songs.
      I listen.

A gentle breeze is rustling
The tops of all the trees—
In unison they're swaying
As their coolness covers me.
      I feel.

I hear the medic 'copter
Flying low across the sky
As it hurries to a center
In hopes that one won't die.
     I pray.

Now and then, I hear a car,
Just an echo down the way—
Too far am I to see it
On this solitary day.
     I'm glad.

The mountains rise above me
Graceful and serene.
So pleased I cannot hear them—
These soundless giants seen—
     I'm grateful.

The day is quickly darkening—
The night will claim the sounds.
And always they'll be there—
But I won't be around.
     I'm sad.

~

July 16, 2002

Sounds in the Night

I hear a creature in my woods;
It's late, too dark to see.
I hear him breathe, not far away—
Perhaps ... can he see me?

Standing still, a bit on guard,
I try to pierce the night.
If only I could see him more,
I'd know that I was right.

A strange and unfamiliar sound
I haven't heard before.
I try to think of something else...
But I hear and can't ignore.

He seems content to stay away,
And so I'm not afraid.
I know the night belongs to him—
That's why the dark was made.

And so I turn to go inside,
Aware of what I know—
That both of us just wanted space
And so let the other go.

May 2000

Miracle among the Animals

In this cold and dirty barn,
A miracle begins—
Deep in the darkened night,
She labors forth her twins.

There's no one there to help her;
There's no one there to see—
But on her own and all alone,
She does it perfectly.

Immediately, she nurtures
Both as they are born—
Protective of the winter's chill,
She tries to keep them warm.

Too soon for them to move about,
She bathes their little heads
And keeps them close beside her
On this hay that makes their bed.

Come morning, they will learn to stand;
Her milk will nourish them.
They will rest throughout this day
In their cozy, little pen.

The mother has to mend her *self*;
There is no doctor near.
Instinctively, she seems to know
How to heal herself out here.

So once again, there's life renewed;
The birth of twins has come,
And they will grow and have their own—
This miracle that's never done.

March 2000

The Cowgirl

She sings to them and whispers *hush,*
But they're skittish, so they turn and rush
First one way and then the next;
She stands alone and quite perplexed.

She dares not move for fear they'll run;
For bravely they are, one–by–one,
Moving closer, closer still
Toward this girl among these hills.

Her voice is soothing, soft and low,
Trying not to make them go.
And slowly they have come to her—
Standing still, she doesn't stir.

One starts to nibble on her clothes—
They're not this trusting, this she knows.
How great they've dared to come this near,
Despite their helpless, inborn fear.

She ever-slowly moves her arm,
They panic, racing 'cross the farm.
It makes her sad to see them leave
But glad of what they've all achieved.

She's certain when she walks again
They'll remember she was once their friend.
And very slowly, slower still,
They'll join her deep within these hills.

~

May 2003

The Miniature Family

They come to eat the food I leave,
My chirping birds of spring.
So small to have such color,
Such fragile little things.

Of late, there's been a blue one,
Like the darkening sky of night.
And a yellow one beside him,
More bright than any light.

Such a miracle of colors,
The Master Painter's touch.
To paint so vividly the birds,
He must love them very much.

Take the time to listen
To a language full of songs.
Every single chirping
To a different bird belongs.

They really do communicate;
You can almost hear them speak.
First one and then another
With their busy little beaks.

A male and then a female
Will mate and make a nest.
From dawn to dusk, they're busy,
And *thank-you, no* to any guests.

And with the nest completed,
The female lays her young.
The male is quite protective
And guards her well from anyone.

The days go by; the eggs are hatched,
And the parent birds are proud.
They chirp to one another
That their little ones are loud.

The sudden need for feeding
Begins and never quits.
Ol' Mom and Dad are tired
And begin to feed in shifts.

What started out as feathers
Is taking shape and form.
Their little squeaks are separate,
Unlike when they were born.

And way too soon, they're bigger;
They fill the tiny nest.
And Mom and Dad are thinking
That *now the time is best.*

Too quickly, they are scooted—
A push and down they go …
Immediately, they're skipping—
Wings take flight, and so …

The little nest is empty
That days ago was filled
With thriving, squirming babies—
And now the nest is still.

There go the male and female;
For now, their job is through.
I wonder: do they stay a pair
Or go on to someone new?

Already I am missing
Their structured, set routine.
A simpler version of ourselves
Is exactly what I've seen.

~

May 2001

Winter Hats

Thank you for this wintry world,
This wonderland of white
That cleanses and refreshes,
Making everything so bright.

I love to see the tumbling snow,
The way it nestles in the trees.
I walk to every window
Just to thrill at what I see.

Deep, and deeper, deepest,
Let everything be dressed
In this glorious wintry white,
Which makes the world look best.

And then the hats—those lovely hats!—
The many hoods of snow:
They cap my little reindeers' heads
That sit atop my porch and glow.

And all along my fencing,
The snow lies calm and still—
An act of balance all its own,
As on my windowsills.

All my plants adorned in white,
Red flowers peeking through
Add just a bit of color,
Just like they always do.

The snow upon our barn roofs
Wear the largest hats of all—
Very flat, yet shapely,
Much like a woman's shawl.

The list goes on forever—
Hats made by winter snow.
And if you've paid attention,
Then you've seen their splendid show!

~

December 2003

IV

A Lantern on Man's Mortality

Seek and Ye Shall Find

There is but one important thought,
One question to be asked.
And surely, on the day we die,
This thought becomes our task.

For when we see our soul escape,
Our only thought should be
Which way to God? Which way is Home?
I'm seeking my eternity.

He likely has a record
Of the deeds we each have done ...
But smiling, I can hear him say
What counts is that you've come.

~

January 1985

Dear Friend

I suffered long, but now I'm free;
To mourn is wrong, for I'm with Thee.
He saw my pain and called me Home
To live again with those I'd known.
Don't be frightened; do not fear—
Your load is lightened when you're Here.
Such peace and joy I can't recall,
No sorrow, pain, or tears at all.
With perfect wisdom one can see
His plan for all Eternity:
At last to know and understand
What still confuses earthly man.

It wasn't hard to pass Beyond
When once I knew my life was gone.
I quickly saw a lighted door,
And there appeared the Holy Lord.
He smiled away my many sins;
Then warmly helped me enter In.
And proudly He did show me round;
Then told me where to settle down.
He said He'd saved this place for me,
And forever this is where I'd be ...

And to my wonder, it did hold
The many things I'd loved of old.
Then suddenly, I realized
When then I dared to meet His eyes,
The me I'd been and known back there,
Before I died and journeyed Here,
Is still the me that stands here now.
For out of love for me, somehow,
He let the treasures of my heart
Be not lost or torn apart.
For all around where I'm to be
Are all the things held dear to me.

And then He said it's time He went
Since now, I knew what Heaven meant.
And anytime I needed Him,
He'd know and quickly step within.
I said how much I felt at home,
Not lost or feeling all alone.
I thanked Him; then He turned to go,
Knowing that I loved Him so.

And so my dear, beloved friend,
My death, you see, was not the end.
Dry your tears; don't weep for me—
I was ... I am ... I'll be ...

~

January 1977—it finally made it, Dad. This one is for you.

Mortal Misgivings

I dare to wish that life was fair,
To reason out from day to day
Those things I read and hear about,
Yet answers still evade my way.
Some are rich and others poor;
Some spend half their lives in school,
While others never learn to read,
Never learning trade or tool.
Still others, taken soon from life—
Snatched away without regard
To age or dreams or talents great—
Their chance at life too quickly charred.
So many really old and worn,
Who rock away their tired souls,
Are anxiously awaiting Him—
Yet still they linger on un-whole.
I advocate chronology—
'Tis right and just and fair.
But I am constantly reminded
How this meets resistance There.
How great to never question,
To believe all things as truth—
Accepting without anger
With a faith as strong as Ruth's.
Such dismay I'm burdened by,
With anger undenied.
So long a way I have to go—
No Christian hero, I.

~

November 1989

The Past

Oh, please let me dwell on the past,
Content in knowing I've *been*—
The future looms large and too iffy,
Wellbeing too distant and dim.

In the past, there was definitely life,
For today, I can see I've survived.
But the future surely holds death—
Will tomorrow still prove me alive?

Yesterday, youth was the victor,
With its sweetness and promise therein.
But age lives on in tomorrows—
At times, more foe than friend.

The past has shown there was time—
And though hours indeed were misspent,
Still, the chance was close within reach
To accomplish whatever I meant.

The future is laced with a panic,
An urgency unknown in the past.
Achievements must quickly be realized:
Still waiting is the day that's our last.

Oh, please let me dwell on the past,
Security and warmth were my friends—
'Twas good to know the familiar,
And safe that it claimed not our end.

February 1989

Onward Seasons, Forward Life

Without good-byes, my spring escaped
Regardless of my grasp.
And now I see my summer's gone
Without a backward glance.

Too quickly, autumn has arrived,
The autumn of my years.
So grieved am I that youth is lost
And left me stranded here.

In harmony with falling leaves
Announcing winter's wake,
I too have glimpsed the changes
That predict my winter breaks.

In peering down the lane ahead,
Too quickly comes a bend;
The road behind is gone for good —
I can't go back again.

The only option feasible
Insists I journey on—
The blinding curve will fall away
When it I come upon.

There, stretching out before me,
Tomorrows, one by one.
I hesitate to hurry
Lest my days be numbered done.

I much prefer the yesteryears—
Indeed, I felt at home.
The future looms precarious,
And I fear its great unknown.

~

October 1990

The Pause of Peace

Anticipating war
With its grim reality.
Soldiers so determined,
Despite their destiny.

Heart-saddened souls at home,
Anxious days and nights
In prayerful consideration
For those prepared to fight.

And thus, opposing nations
Each committed to its cause
Await relentless leaders
In this momentary pause.

An agonizing pause it is,
The calm before a storm.
While leaders bid and bargain
To keep a war unborn.

The fate of many thousands
Depends on choices made,
On whether peace will reigneth
Or terms of war are laid.

Someone must relinquish:
A leader, nation, cause—
In order for survival
To live beyond this pause.

Which challenge is the nobler—
Charging forward mid the strife
Or backing off in sure defeat
To save a human life?

~

January 13, 1991

Christmas Passing

Christmas Passing

To leave us here on Christmas Day
With broken hearts and wondering why …
Of all the time to go away,
Of all the days to bid good-bye.
Our grieving souls are deep in pain,
So blinded by these endless tears.
If only you could come again,
If only you could join us here.

But *is* it such an awful thing
For *him* who must depart,
To see, firsthand, the angels sing
Their carols on such holy harps?
For surely at this time of year,
A wreath is hung with care
On Heaven's door to beckon near
Those whose journey takes them There.

And maybe just inside its Gates
There stands so great a tree—
And perched within its branches wait
Snow-white doves for all to see.
Atop its leaves are silver bells
That never cease to ring—
They have a message for to tell
And this they seem to sing.

And there upon its highest limb
There stands a brilliant star—
The one that shone o'er Bethlehem
To guide those from afar.
But Here it shines forevermore,
And still to mark the Place
Where we can go to yet adore
The One who dwells in Awe and Grace.
Perhaps inside—such brilliant lights
Do surely deck the halls
To reassure there is no Night
While spreading warmth to all.

And there sits He whose birthday is
Remembered o'er the earth;
And Here such joy it seems is His,
While all recall His Holy birth.
For surely Heaven celebrates
In a way we've never seen—
Such rejoicing inside its Gates
Is more than we could dream.
For such an honor it must be
To be called to pass that Way—
A chosen one, and thus to see
Heaven's joy on Christmas Day.

~

Christmas 1984

The Visitors

Great shock and disbelief
Did visit us today.
How I wish they hadn't come,
But instead had stayed away.

We really weren't prepared—
Our minds preoccupied
With earthly things about us,
It caught us by surprise.

Such worry and concern
For the one we hold so dear
Has consumed our daily thinking
Since the visitor was here.

But something else has happened,
I feel it more and more—
It seems another visitor
Has journeyed through our door.

After grief and anger
Become a set routine,
Quietly, compassion
Sneaks in upon the scene.

Other people's problems
Become more quickly real.
Suddenly, you're well aware
The pain you know they feel.

Ironic how it happens—
Appears as though 'tis planned:
How grief and then compassion
Do enter hand in hand.

~

March 1988

Many years ago, my daughter, Anna, lost one of her best friends. It was an extremely painful and difficult time for Anna and she had a hard time getting through it all. These next three poems are in memory of Tonya and for Anna.

Winter's Flower

A car, a curve, a chilling fog,
Spoken words, a look, a nod ...
Crashing metal, nothing left,
A sickening silence—death.

An hour come, an hour gone,
A tender life unjustly wronged.
Within that hour comes an end,
Someone's daughter, someone's friend.

Very lovely, sweet as spring,
But 'twas the winter with its sting
That now forbids her cheerful play,
Forbids her youth these summer days.

A flower just about to bloom;
Then swiftly plucked away too soon—
A flower sad that winter came
And in the mist, it breathed her name.

~

June 1994—for love of Tonya.

And Then I Wake, and You Are Gone

In my dreams, I see you, alive and still so young,
Always gaily laughing and having so much fun.
Your eyes are dancing merrily; your face has such a glow,
And I am so excited, since (for now) I do not know ...
And then I wake, and you are gone.

In my dreams, I see you, and I am also there,
And once again, we're doing all those things we used to share.
Such joy to be together, as though we'd never been apart—
Two adoring friendships that bonded from the start.
And then I wake, and you are gone.

In my dreams, I see you, and in one, I tried to hint
Of great impending danger, but you wouldn't be convinced.
Your determination soothed me; I decided I was wrong,
For here you were beside me, alive and well and strong.
And then I wake, and you are gone.

In my dreams, I see you—I'm overcome with such relief,
It means it didn't happen, and my joy's beyond belief.
Our lives still lie ahead—and intertwined, as we had planned,
Each one forever willing to reach out and lend her hand.
And then I wake, and you are gone.

In my dreams, I see you, but I must learn to let you go,
I cannot keep on meeting you in a place that isn't so.
The pain upon awakening, the intensely bitter sorrow,
The realization that, for us, there's no tomorrow.
And when I wake, you're surely gone.

In my dreams, I see you, but my dreams need sadly cease,
They haunt me; I'm afraid to sleep, and can't find any peace.
You know I'll always love you; and a part of you is me,
But I must say good-bye until our souls are running free.
And when I wake, I'll let you go.

~

November 1995—for Anna and Tonya

One Last Time

Cleanse me from this sorrow;
Erase from me this grief.
Two years since—and still tomorrow
Holds the threat of no relief.

A creek of tears has spilled away—
With never any end
It keeps on flowing on its way
Round and round my soul again.

One person's life, another's death—
The two cannot be one.
Accepting that they've gone and left
Sometimes can't be done.

And what about the living
If peace cannot be found;
If thoughts are unrelenting
Of those no longer round?

Grant to me an hour
To be near to you again.
Please request this power
Oh, my beloved friend.

Let me look upon your face
And see your smile once more.
Let me one more time embrace
This friend I so adore.

I long to hear you laughing
And see that you survived
Beyond the wall of dying
And are safe and still alive.

I need for you to teach me
That your memory is enough
To keep me smiling when I'm happy
And get me through when times are tough.

I beg of you to help me
Get beyond those days in March;
Convince me I can now be free
Of grief alone and in the dark.

Persuade me just to ponder
Your life and not your death,
To remember days of yonder
Instead of what is left.

Remind me that we'll play again,
And then, with no good-byes.
Time to be together when
I will never need to cry.

Come back and tell me all these things,
Allow my heart to know.
Let me kiss your tiny wings
And then, I'll let you go.

~

March 1996—for Anna and Tonya

Forever Gone or Going On

The fury came with blinding force,
Never seen by all mankind.
And every soul felt such remorse
To witness this—the end of time.

There came a speeding hail of fire
Intercepting Earth today.
And all the world became a choir
As every culture paused to pray.

For most, just precious hours left.
Thousands flee, and others stay:
Too young, too old, too sick to let
The thought of death decide their way.

A chance so slim, 'tis doubtful
To halt impending death—
But still the world is hopeful,
And united, holds its breath.

A brave and daring, knowing cast
Has devised a risky plan
To try and stop a second blast
And save the doom of man.

But should they be successful
It will mean they lose their lives.
Still, they're honored to be able
To give it one last try.

The time is early afternoon,
Already millions gone.
The world awaits its verdict soon—
Will man go down or life go on?

~

February 1999—based on the movies *Armageddon* and *Deep Impact*

Down Whisper Road

One very early summer's morn
Before the darkness turned to light
He drove his truck down Whisper Road
And there he took his life.

An hour passed between the time
He stopped his truck, then died.
An hour to a tortuous soul
And no one heard his cries.

He drove his truck down Whisper Road
Like many times before.
He passed familiar homes and farms
Not to see them anymore.

Did doubt become his torment?
Did remorse become his jail?
Along the way on Whisper Road
Did he hope perhaps he'd fail?

Arriving at the place he'd planned
His fight raged on an hour.
Only he himself was there
And his own destructive power.
One very early summer's morn
Before the darkness turned to light
He drove his truck down Whisper Road
And there he took his life.

~

September 1997

The Funeral

Silently they stand o'er me;
Momma's dressed in black,
And Daddy's got his best suit on—
He mostly doesn't dress like that.

The sun is bright; the day is warm;
The time of year is fall.
They seem relieved the weather's fine—
I know it matters not at all.

Family, friends, and relatives
Have come to bid me well
On this, my final journey,
Since I've shed my outer shell.

And what a shell it was to shed,
Diseased and racked with pain.
What a blessed gift it is
To be alive again.

They seem perplexed, not knowing how
To handle this, their grief—
They know that they will miss me
But rejoice in my relief.
I too have buried others dear
And cried that they were gone.
But now I see and know firsthand
They were with us all along.

They know it really isn't me
They've rested 'neath the earth,
But that my soul has gone beyond
And claimed its second birth.

But still I long to tell them
I am hovering right above,
Suspended close beside them
And can feel their pain and love.

I want to hold each one again
And bid them not to doubt,
To send them off in warmth and light,
Revealing what it's all about.
In tears, they've turned to sadly go,
The service now complete.
But as for me, I'm glad to leave:
There are angels still to meet.

~

September 1995

Scattered Flowers

Where have all the flowers gone,
The trees with all their leaves?
The birds aren't singing cheerful songs;
The days so quickly leave.
Children playing merrily,
Young mothers in the park—
Their days are brightly shining,
Mine are fringed with shadows dark.
The newlyweds are starry-eyed;
Then with babies newly born.
Was I ever one of them?
Have I always been this worn?
I used to see a mountain,
But now it's just a hill.
A wide and rushing river
Is now a stream that's almost still.
The thoughts of my tomorrows
Brought smiles upon my face.
But now my brow is fearful,
With sadness set in place.
Where have all the flowers gone?
They wilted, blew away.
For they were part of what was youth
That dropped on by but couldn't stay.

~

January 1999

Nightingale in White

His pain was so intense;
His eyes were filled with tears.
She was quickly by his side,
When she heard him call her near.

Gentle hands and soothing words,
A pill to ease his plight.
He lifted up a weary smile
To his nightingale in white.

He knows his time is drawing near;
He's afraid to be alone.
So in his deepest, darkest night,
She's his friend away from home.

She doesn't have to say a lot,
She can't make things all right.
With compassion, though, she listens
As his nightingale in white.

He voices many quiet fears,
With questions now and then.
She answers with her knowledge
And knows to not pretend.
The pill has eased his pain a bit,
And in the evening light
He asks to know a bit about
His nightingale in white.

She wisely tells him certain things,
Omitting many more.
She knows his life is ending,
With hers an open door.

Instead, she quickly centers back
And asks about his life.
He only wants to thank her
That she's his nightingale in white.

He's tired now and wants to sleep
But hates for her to go.
Assuring him she'll stay awhile,
He presumes her night is slow.
She thinks his sleep is peaceful,
But he barely clings to life.
So his head she gently kisses—
This nightingale in white.

~

November 1998—for love of Anna ... our nurse.

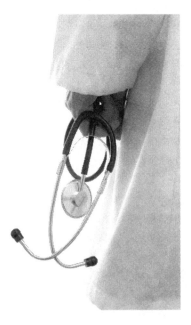

September 11, 2001

I heard a pastor say today
One person died three thousand times;
It helped to make more personal
Three thousand deaths they'll never find.

Such barbaric acts upon us;
The world is filled with rage.
Yet for everyone who perished,
Their lives can only fill a page.

And even so, the book is heavy—
Too much reading to be done.
Instead, they stay within our hearts
Where we remember each as *one*.

For each there was a life worth living,
Loved by families, loved by friends.
Then, in less than just an hour,
All these *ones* had faced their end.

Every someone had a history,
Years of growing, dreams, and goals.
Then so quickly, all have vanished,
Denied the chance of growing old.

The innocent were terrorized,
As we were helpless but to see
How such an ordinary day
Could end so tragically.

The world has vowed to not forget
Regardless of tomorrows
How on this day in mid-September,
We stood as one in all our sorrow.

~

October 2001

Her Torment

A little girl is called to heaven—
A car wreck and she's gone.
The mother lives but longs to die:
Where's the reason for going on?

The little girl becomes an angel—
One of heaven's chosen few.
But left behind the mother grieves
For this little girl she knew.

The little girl knows happiness
Even greater since she's died.
But her mother's torment continues
Without her daughter by her side.

There may be ecstasy beyond
For this little girl of nine.
But her mother's left to suffer
For an eternity of time.

~

January 2001

Dark Hours

Dark Hours

She lay on her bed with her heart full of sorrow,
Holding her husband; there would be no tomorrow.
His body now free from what took his life,
She held him and waited deep through the night.

They were coming to take him where each of us goes
At the time in our life when we no longer know.
But there on their bed with moments so few,
She lay in her grief of what they would do.

The last time to have him so close by her side,
To touch him and kiss him with no one nearby.
In the quiet-filled room, she was blessed with the time
To say her good-byes as he left her behind.

In the dark, she remembered the life they had shared,
Short as it was, for they hadn't been spared.
But love isn't measured only by years—
As strong as was theirs, he would always be near.

She knew he was gone, but reminisced on;
She would cry and say it was wrong
That he had to go and she had to stay;
And why did he have to be taken away?

She could feel her broken, pounding heart
As she knew so soon they'd be apart.
She wanted to go and bolt the door
And stay beside him forever more.

But that she knew could never be
So she held him close, so lovingly.
Each precious moment slipped on by
While she talked and hugged, kissed, and cried.

The awful sound she'd been waiting for,
That dreaded knocking at their door,
So painfully had finally come—
Their last together time was done …

The room they shared was empty, bare—
The one she loved no longer there.
She lay alone upon their bed
And pretended she could hold his head.

~

June 2003—with heartfelt compassion for the wife who did this.

Hanging On

She's hanging on, all this time,
So much pain, a weary mind.
Gone the life she used to know
And yet denied the right to go.

She's fought the fight, and even more—
No longer who she was before.
The spark of life forever gone,
And yet, and still, she's hanging on.

A gentlewoman, quiet, kind,
A lonely widow left behind—
One whose faith grew deep with years,
One who took to God her tears.

Her days are numbered, most are gone;
Some say her suffering's gone too long.
She would say God isn't wrong,
And that is why I'm holding on.

Since Christmas is upon us,
How great if gracious Jesus
Would come and take her far away
To be with Him on Christmas Day.

~

December 2004—for love of Joannie

Request to Enter

I question, I doubt, I get angry, I pout,
Awful things happen, I get sad, I get mad.
I don't understand, such grief in our hands,
You could have said no, but You let it be so.

Loved ones are taken, our souls are left shaken,
Our lives are disrupted, routines interrupted.
We cry, then we wail, we curse when things fail,
Where is our God, when He gives such a nod?

Through lots of our fears, we don't feel You near,
We want You nearby, but You're too high in the sky.
Our scared hearts are sad for fear You'll be mad
That we pushed You away when You wanted to stay.

We believe, then we don't, we hope, then we won't,
A merry-go-round that can't settle down.
I know You're disgusted that we just can't be trusted,
Our faith is so hollow, we can't seem to follow.

But God, I am guilty of all the above—
I've used the word we, but mostly it's *me*.
And now, Lord, I'm asking, forgive me my sins,
And then when I die, won't You please let me In?

~

December 2003

Unborn Soul

A soul that's never born,
A little one conceived—
A brokenhearted woman
Has lost the one she needs.

Where goes this unborn baby,
This child that never grows?
Someone's hopes and dreams
They never get to know.

Is it gone and lost forever
Or returned from whence it came?
Surely, God recovers
These tiny ones, unnamed.

They're every bit as precious
As healthy babies born—
They're every bit as loved
And every one, we mourn.

They're important little beings,
Though just a while they came—
I *know* that God recovers
These tiny ones, unnamed.

~

January 2009—for women everywhere

V

A Lantern on Philosophy, Life, and Self

My Song

I'll sing a song
Of right and wrong,
Of joy and love
Or Him above.

I'll sing of fear
Or danger near.
I'll sing of wants
Or that which haunts.

I'll sing a song
To one that longs
For lasting peace
And wars to cease.

I'll sing to those
With spirits low.
I'll make them rise
With shining eyes.

To those grown old
Whose lives are sold …
I'd sing to bless
These souls at rest.

And to a child
So young and wild …
I'd sing with joy
To a little boy.

To those in pain,
Who live in vain,
I'll sing with praise
For healthy days.

In Heaven, on Earth,
For all that I'm worth,
Where 'ere I belong
I'll sing my song.

~

Mid 1960s—written in fun.

The Answers Lie

Don't ask me why the sun is gold
Or why the sky is blue.
Don't ask me why leaves tend to fold
Or why the flowers blossom anew.

Don't ask me why the birds can sing
Or why the insects crawl.
Don't ask me why our church bells ring
Or why the stars can fall.

Ask me not of the fish that swarm the seas,
Or of animals that roam the lands.
Ask me not of men who try to flee,
To find free lives as their dreams have planned.

Ask me not such questions for which you demand,
For you'll find that I won't reply.
'Cause the answers lie in God's Master Plan,
And there they'll stay as time goes by.

~

Mid 1960s

Thoughts of a Young Soldier

He was just a young boy, not much a man,
When he kissed his mom goodbye and shook his father's hand.
As he turned to board the train, he waved a last good-bye,
And a tear rolled down his cheek as he saw his sister cry …

He chose a seat at the rear of the car;
He was going alone, and he was going far.
Still a boy of just nineteen,
Full of life and full of dreams …

He remembered when younger, he used to pretend
That he shot the bad guy—a hero again!
But now it was different, 'cause this was no game—
Fighting a real war was just not the same …

He longed to be home and back with the guys,
Going to parties and getting high.
Whistling at girls while speeding through town—
Those were the days he was longing for now …

But soon, the brakes began to screech, the whistle then was blown;
This must have been the shortest trip that he had ever known.
Jerked back into the present time, he gathered up his things
And headed for the camp that he knew not what would bring …

The days and weeks have come and gone,
And the whole world seems to lie beyond
These wretched walls that make a camp,
Equipped with barracks, cold, and damp …

The smile he wore has been replaced
By hard, taut lines about his face.
His careless, awkward ways are gone—
His boyish body now made strong …

They've taught him how to hate and kill—
They've made him hard against his will.
His once kind heart has turned to steel—
Now he sees, but does not feel.

Here in action, his war has begun.
As machine guns are fired, the enemy runs.
With his rifle in hand, on his belly he crawls
Through the mud and the filth, till finally he falls …

His face is unshaven and scarred so it bleeds—
Scraped from the briars, the sticks, and the weeds.
He rolls in the mud with the grace of a boar
As he thinks to himself, *this* is the war …

He sees someone move from behind a near brush,
He triggers his rifle and gives it a push.
He panics, then shoots—sight unseen,
And prays to God at the morbid scream …

As he parts the thicket, his tears are a flood,
The enemy lies dead in a pool of blood.
For here was a man who minutes ago
Had wanted to live—little did he know …

To a soldier at war, life isn't worthwhile
When fallen men are dead in piles.
A bullet is fired, another one dies,
And the others trudge on while asking *Why?*

For those who die had hopes and dreams
Of living life the way it seems
Life should be lived. And yet they fall
Before they have a chance at all …

The soldier prays for a ray of light
To guide him on, but he must fight.
Not knowing if he'll lose his place—
He finds it hard to keep his faith …

He wants to think he was born to live—
To love and learn, to share and give.
He does not want to die alone,
Still so young and far from home …

Yet this is what the others wished,
But now they're gone; they don't exist.
And so he asks will he be spared,
And why, when all the others cared?

He wonders if the world beyond
Really knows what all goes on.
They read the headlines, watch the news,
But no one wins, for both sides lose …

He thinks about his own small role
Compared to all as a whole.
He feels the war would be the same,
If they'd never even seen his name …

The months have dwindled, one by one
And the time for him to leave has come.
He's served his time, and he's served it well—
What lies ahead he cannot tell …

The ride back home was long and slow—
Unlike the one so long ago.
He thought the trip was worth his while,
For his heavy thoughts could pass the miles …

Here he is a'heading home,
But his friends are left back there alone.
Again, he asks why he's been spared,
But now he doesn't seem to care …

He knows how young he was back then,
When life was bad, he could just pretend.
But now he's seen through tear-stained eyes
The part of life he once disguised …

Again, he'll shake his father's hand,
This time, though, he'll be a man—
If killing means you outgrow toys,
He'd just as soon have stayed a boy ...

As he saw the station up the track,
He turned to get his army hat—
This time he smiled, instead of sighed,
When he saw his sister start to cry ...

~

Late 1960s, when in high school.

Lone Beggar Man

Lone Beggar Man

Forceful wind rips through the night.
Small, freezing raindrops fill the air.
It's late; It's dark—the only light
Is from a lamppost over there.

There's a darkened alley ... this part of town:
Vacant. Dirty. Lonely.
Decent folks don't come around—
For dropouts, beggars only.

The jagged street with broken glass
Is hard on shoeless feet.
The puddles, filled with mud—alas!—
Accommodate the falling sleet.

Scampering mice do not await
The cat, well known, with sharp clawed feet
And slanted eyes. They won't be bait
For him that prowls along the street.

A ragged, poor man on the corner
Sits beneath the lamppost light.
He's happy. He's the owner
Of this alley—late at night.

A worn-out coat with holes and threads—
A rotting stick, his cane;
The jagged street—his nighttime bed
Despite the wind, the freezing rain.

This beggar man—it's only guest,
The alley, vacant stays.
No one nears the poor man's nest;
No one cares to know his ways.

Each night—whatever it be:
Rain. Sleet. Snow.
The old man sits, stares, and sees
The darkened street, again, alone.

Sunrise, he rises. Goes.
Rotting cane, and feebled feet.
To where? But no one knows.
At night, he's back again on alley street.

~

Summer 1970

Lost

Life without breath,
Day without night,
Birth without death—
      Lost.

A storm without rain,
A star by itself,
All clouds just the same—
      Lost.

A tree without leaves,
A hill with no height,
Things such as these—
      Lost.

Birds that can't fly,
Bees that can't sting,
To exist without sky—
      Lost.

A child with no home,
A man with no name—
Both are alone—
      Lost.

To have not a goal,
Nothing to grasp.
A lonely soul—
      Lost.

To live and then die
But never remembered,
To forever lie—
      Lost.

∼

August 1972

Thank-You Very Kindly Sir

Get on your feet, America,
And hear what I have to say:
Don't criticize a man who tries
To speak for the American Way.

Times are tough; the goods are few,
And the world is well aware.
I think we're lucky, me and you,
To have a friend out there.

If a countryman, though not our own,
Should write in our behalf,
To make a friendly feeling known—
Just who are we to laugh?

Since when have we considered
Ourselves a land to be
Far too great and much too proud
To acknowledge graciously?

If someone wants to compliment
Or stand and say a word for us—
I'd like to know just where it went:
This thing called humbleness.

It's said of us that we possess
What other lands desire.
But do they want such snobbishness
That comes when all's acquired?

I should think we can still be proud
Of this country we call home,
And yet, with heads so humbly bowed,
Be glad for praises not our own.

I, for one, am not ashamed
Of the praises to which I refer.
And to the gentleman, may I proclaim:
We thank you very kindly, sir!

~

January 1974

Richard Milhous Nixon

How great is the man who resigned with a grace
That not many of us can possess.
To be forced out of office with dignity erased:
What more can one man, alone, face?

Such is a man that our country has known,
And such is a man that is lost.
We'd do well to remember the good he has sewn
And forget any wrong that was tossed.

He ended our war with the peace that we asked
And fought till our soldiers were home.
At the time, we rejoiced, but it just didn't last,
For ingratitude is now what we've shown.

We've kicked him and mocked him and beaten him down,
And stripped him of dignity too.
For now, we have taken his home and his town,
Forbidding him the life that he knew.

He's fought the good fight, but only to lose
The battle for what he believed.
For finally we've said that at last he must choose
To die standing up or to leave.

A man's just a man; how important he be
Matters not if the world turns away.
For what has he left, if he turns round to see
His own soul being drowned in the bay?

His voice didn't quiver, and his smile didn't hide
As he quietly stepped down from his throne.
He wished the world well and stepped gracefully aside—
This man who is now so alone.

Often we find the good that was missed
Too late to say we were wrong.
Perhaps someday our country will wish
To put a great man where he belongs.

~

August 1974

Sleep

I need to go to sleep now
For I am tired so.
I need to go to sleep now
And lay my head down low.

How I hate I must surrender
To this sleep that's calling me—
How I hate I must surrender
To the night's serenity.

There's so much else that I could do
If wakefulness were mine—
There's so much else that I could do
But I've run out of time.

Must I let go this precious peace
I find so late at night?
Thus will go the precious peace
When out I turn my light …

~

June 1984

The Diary

Like the waves upon the shore
That go rushing out to sea,
Our days and months and years
Rush away from you and me.
What was once a day ago
Will tomorrow be a year—
Our daily lives so quickly gone,
Taking moments held so dear.
Those yesterdays cannot return,
Except for in our minds—
And those we just cannot recall
Are lost forever, left behind.

But why not keep a journal
And daily write it down?
Then those lost-forever moments
Could so easily be found.
Is not the time worth spending
To safely guard our past?
For tomorrow comes too quickly,
And today will go too fast.

~

June 1987

A Reason

Disbelief, heartache, grief, and despair,
Much pain to endure, such crosses to bear.
Anxiety, confusion, animosity, feuds,
Mortality for certain, a brief interlude.
Where lies the beauty that makes it worthwhile?
In the midst of life's chaos, a little child smiles.

~

February 1988

On-the-Go Prayers

Early in the morning and again late at night
I mostly seem too tired, Lord,
To pray with strength and might.
So I'm hoping You're accepting
My prayers throughout the day—
They're short and interrupted,
Yet sincere in what they say.
They often have no ending,
I rarely say *Amen,*
Yet, Lord, I hope You're listening
When I go to speak again.

~

February 1988

Postponed Pleasure

If we work before we pleasure,
Making sure our tasks are done,
We'll only be rewarded
If that time for pleasure comes.

But what if we discover,
When we see our work is through
And go to seek enjoyment,
That the day has ended, too?

We should strive to find a balance,
Insisting every day,
When done with all our labors,
To claim the pleasure we delayed.

~

February 1988

And from this Web, the Dew

This woeful web of dailiness
That comes to plague us all
Must exist to catch the dew
That sometimes sweetly falls.

There's never any way to know
If, amid our grueling day,
There'll come a moment so exquisite,
We pause to see it pass our way.

And should we be unwilling
Each day to persevere,
Our blinded eyes would fail to see
The dew that may have settled near.

So often, it is silent,
Unnoticed by the rest;
Below an office window,
A robin builds her nest.
How great the chance to be above—
Where oft' we are below—
To view the birth of baby birds
And then to watch them grow.

Or maybe on a wintry day,
A cold and snowy morn,
You marvel how the world is dressed
In virgin white throughout the storm.

And just as gently as the dew
Drifts in to settle round,
Perhaps a friend should chance to say
A word to turn your frown.

Or maybe on a busy day
Amid a set routine—
There, suddenly, the hand of God
You know you felt, unseen.
And with great appreciation
You marvel how He cared.
The warmth you felt in knowing that
In all the world, He saw *you* there.

And so come hence, you woeful web;
Do spin yourself anew.
Come hither unto me each day
And I will catch your dew!

~

May 1984

My Lake

I take a walk each afternoon
And pass this certain lake;
Everyday it's different though
With changes that it makes.

At times, it looks a murky brown,
Debris strewn all about;
Not even fish would surface there—
"Too hazardous!" they'd shout.

Next day, when out I go again
I marvel that I see
A lake so clean and shimmering—
Reflecting trees ... and me.

Perhaps the lake is moody
Like those who pass it by.
At times, its ripples still and clear,
At peace with earth and sky.

But like its human counterpart,
It has its dismal days,
When "life is not so beautiful,"
I hear her waters say.

Alas, tomorrow always comes—
Each day, another chance.
Perhaps I'll see contentment
Upon her waters dance.

And maybe, then she'll notice
A lighter step in me ...
How nice, the days we mirror
Each other's harmony.

~

December 1982

Duo Depresso

When we're down in the dumps
And feeling blue,
You come to me,
And I'll go to you.
For both of us know
Where the other is at:
We've been there ourselves
And found the way back.
We're feeling too fat;
Our hair is a mess!
Our makeup's outdated—
Should I finish the rest?
We hate the whole world—
But mostly ourselves.
How good it would be
To stand up and yell!
How good it would be
To leave things behind,
To get us together,
To gripe and to whine.
To go somewhere special
And pig out till we burst—
Then cry to each other
That we've made ourselves worse!
Then, maybe we'd feel
Our moods drain away,
And figure it time
To call it a day.
To see ourselves selfish—
Ungrateful by far—
And then be determined
To like what we are.
But this little visit
Can't come to be—
I can't go to you
Or you come to me.

Blest be to the phone—
A minute away.
How good we can hear
What our hearts want to say.
Never mind all the miles,
The distance apart—
We'll call when we're blue
And air out our hearts!

~

January 1985—for Janice and me

Progression of Time

1.

I've been searching for a Time
That's been difficult to find.
Time for me, time for you,
Time for me to be with you.

Uninterrupted hours,
Longer lasting days,
Time for one another
When an hour longer stays.

More time to spend on only me,
With obligations few,
Pursuing buried interests
I lacked the time to do.

And you, my dear, my greatest love,
Will ever there be time
For you to sit and contemplate,
With worries far behind?

I foresee that down the road
This Time will come along ...
But there, I see I'm troubled,
And I fear that something's wrong ...

2.

My mirror's looking different—
Though I've had it many years—
Could that be *myself* I see:
A face with many tears?

It seems that Time has found a friend;
I'd forgotten that it had:
It took away the youthful me,
And now at times I'm sad.

I know I've heard its name before—
I think they call it Age;
They say that it's the Book of Life,
And every year's a page.
And now I have that wanted Time
I strived so hard towards.
But I catch myself reflecting
On memories long since stored.

Hours seem too silent
With little voices still.
Is not this what I longed for,
When those voices tried my will?

It seems we're never satisfied,
Never quite content.
The young will wish they're older,
Their lives more quickly spent.

Then maybe on arrival
To those quiet, golden years—
We turn around at times and miss
Those days no longer here.

3.
My Book of Life's half over;
My page reads early fall.
I wonder if I'm wise enough
Not to hurry it at all.

I still hear little voices;
My house holds tiny feet.
Many days I'm void of time,
With commitments still to keep.

Yet I've made myself a promise:
To enjoy this page I'm on,
To live it to its fullest
And not to wish it gone.

If this I do successfully,
Then down that golden road—
Without remorse or great regrets,
I'll accept the lighter load.

And then will start another page;
And though it's near the end,
My Book of Life will be renewed
When my Eternity begins.

~

January 20, 1988

Hidden Victors

People hurting people
In cruel, destructive ways,
Causing insult to the body
While its owner lies afraid.

Children hurting children
In cruel, destructive ways.
Undaunted, unremorseful
Of the seeds of hurt they lay.

The older harm the body,
But children hurt the mind.
Regarding other's feelings,
They're deaf and dumb and blind.

I worry what will happen
If the youth I see today
Don't change before tomorrow
But keep their hurtful ways.

Tomorrow they'll be older;
Tomorrow they'll be grown.
Yesterday they thought it cool
To hurt their very own.

They really need to hurry—
The time is growing late.
They have so long a way to go
To change this awful state.

It really does surprise me
Why they hurt each other so.
Their biting words are painful;
Their mocking ways are low.

They tease, harass, belittle,
Poke fun at every turn.
They haven't any morals—
'Least not that I discern.

Why can't they stick together
And help each other out;
Get through these years together
Making easier their route?

The few that seem most able
To decipher right from wrong,
Barred from youth's society—
They simply don't belong.

Their road is long and lonely;
Not many will they pass.
This *rightful* path, however
Is the only one that lasts.

Their many other peers,
Walking roads away from them,
Will someday sadly see
The road they're on dead ends.

And then these outcast few,
Who were scorned a while ago,
When they see their peers have fallen
Will come to surely know:

Indeed, that isolated road
They chose to walk alone
Has given them the victory,
A better life to own.

~

March 1988—for my daughter, Anna, and her sisters, Melanie and
Meghan, who later followed in her footsteps.

My Successor

Must descendent generations
Succeed us quite so soon?
It hardly seems so long ago
'Twas we who sought to bloom.

The child we bore while in our youth
Is now more youth than child.
When next we know he'll bear his own
Will seem but just a while.

I am constantly reminded—
When I see her on the go—
That once upon a time 'twas I
Who frolicked to and fro.

The sparkle dancing in her eyes,
Her golden tumbling mane,
The beauty of her youthfulness
Were all once mine to claim.

Her everyday adventures,
The things I see her do,
Forever I'm remembering
The younger me I knew.

And so this generation
Too quickly did appear.
And to my daughter, my successor,
I humbly pass youth's mirror.

~

June 1989

Accepting Self

Self-esteem,
It hardly seems
Should so impose
To cause such woes.
And yet it can ...

Problems great
Untimely fate—
Each one's endured
When self's assured.
Indeed, it's true ...

Contented days
Do mark your way;
Though all may fail,
Your self prevails,
And you survive ...

The yeas and nays
The world might say—
Not always needed
Nor often heeded—
You need them not.

You judge *yourself,*
And nothing else
Nor those around
Can bring you down—
Only you.

But even so,
Those flaws you know
You just conclude
Are part of you.
And you accept.

How great t'would be
To claim for me
A self at ease
And mostly pleased.
How good indeed.

~

August 1989 for CM

Acceptance

The insecurities of self
That just won't go away,
It seems, must be accepted
For some are here to stay.

If self cannot be altered,
The will too strongly set,
The only one alternative
Is simply to accept.

One comfort still remains
To staid ourselves upon:
Perhaps we judge too harshly
These flaws we wish were gone.

If others be less bothered,
Not troubled by our quirks,
We only have ourselves to face—
Our source of greatest hurt.

~

January 1988

Deceitful Imagery

We love to let each other down;
Our imperfections do abound.
Our mirror image isn't true:
It only shows how you see you.
For that reflection which we see—
The one we view as surely me—
Is oftentimes conceited praise,
A dream of what we'd like portrayed.
The rest of us are not as kind:
Another's faults and flaws we find.
How shocked we'd be if we but knew
That mirror image isn't true!

We love to let each other down,
To scatter expectations round.
To shatter little daily dreams—
The kind that build one's self esteem.
We're always busy with ourselves,
So thoughtfulness must then be shelved.
Kind and friendly niceties
Don't make it to reality.
We're destined to procrastinate—
Then turn to find the hour late.
The opportunity, then, is missed—
Thoughtfulness, once more, a wish.

And so we let each other down;
Our lack of love goes round and round.
If mirror images could be true—
Our good reflection would shine on you.

~

October 1984

Silent Hurts

Perhaps I've hurt you
And know it not.
I hear your silence,
Which hurts a lot.
Your disregard
Where once 'twas not,
Your cool response
Indeed I've caught.
If wrong I've done
It wasn't meant;
If wronged you felt,
Your silence sent
Has surely pained.
But I will not
Be hurt again.
Now I know
What not to do
To keep from hurting
Me … or you.

~

March 1988

Remember When

Broken treasures, broken stones,
Broken hearts, and broken bones.
What can make them whole again—
Or must we just remember when?

Broken friendships, broken homes,
Saddened people left alone.
What can make them whole again—
Or must they just remember when?

Nothing stays forever long;
Eventually all things are gone.
And yes, we're left remembering when,
Content in knowing it *has been*.

~

April 1988

Illusions

Although the sky seems blue, 'tis not.
And do we see the wind a lot?
We don't. For only in the swaying trees
Is shown the wind to you and me.

A mountain looming far and still
Would seem to be but o'er that hill.
When oft' we hope that something's near,
We sadly learn 'twas never here.

If dare I seek to read your heart,
Because I've known you from the start,
Invariably, I'll read you wrong
While sure I knew you all along.

And wonder I how well we know
The part of us that never shows.
How deep goes truth till fantasy
Disguises true reality?

~

April 1988

Pondering

What would you do with the rest of your life
If you had but a day left on earth?
Would you wallow in grief, turn inward in strife,
Maybe contemplate your worth?

Would you bargain with God in order to live,
Vowing promises unable to keep:
"To all of the world myself I will give,"
On bended knees, would you weep?

Might you fly in a panic to places unseen,
Desperately attempting to try
At least to say that there you've been—
Though 'tis just before you die?

Maybe contentment would keep you at home—
A familiar routine to pursue
With family and friends around that you've known
And avoiding anything new.

So what would you do if you had but a day?
A really tough question I pose—
Perhaps the best answer is simply to say,
'Tis good that we don't have to know!

~

February 1989

Choices

Sometimes the hardest days in life
Are when you hear those chanting voices
That look you squarely in the eye,
Saying *Yes, you have these choices.*
They do not tell you what to do;
They offer no advice,
Except to say, *Please hurry up,*
A decision would be nice!
But that is not so easy,
I say to all these voices.
So, thank-you much, but go away
And take with you your choices!

~

November 1988

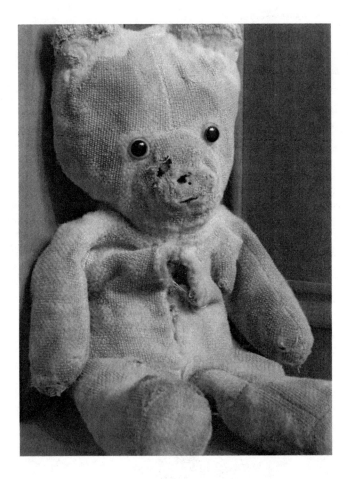

The Antique Upon the Shelf

I sit up here upon this shelf,
Collecting dust and webs.
Not quite so often needed,
They put me here instead.

Now and then, they take me down
When they have need of me—
'Tis then that they remember
How useful I can be.

They handle me with tenderness;
They'd die were I to break.
I'm valued very highly,
But less often as of late.

My contribution over,
They have finished with myself—
And now so ever gently,
They return me to my shelf.

~

April 1994

In Search of Song

Once upon a time ago,
Lived a bird who couldn't sing.
Though he spent long hours trying,
Not a chirp did stir his wings.

He had wrongly built his nest
In a grove of many trees.
So thick the woods around him,
He couldn't feel the breeze.

Other feathered friends
Had built their nests nearby.
Soon the bird felt stifled,
Yet no one heard his cry.

But then the wise and friendly owl
Did notice his despair
And cautiously suggested
That he move away from there.

He wondered to the little bird,
"Might the absence of your song
Coincide with discontent—
Might you feel you don't belong?"

Agreeing with his friend, the owl,
Uprooting thus his nest,
He bid his feathered friends adieu—
Then off to find his quest.

On he flew, for half a day
Until his watchful eye
Spotted such a quiet place,
He couldn't pass it by.

There he saw a stately oak
Perched high atop a hill—
It stood alone in solitude
With branches full and still.

He knew at once his flight was done,
'Tis here he'd settle in.
And so with great contentment,
He built his nest again.

So happy was the little bird
Secure within this tree—
He chirped away in blissful song
That here he loved to be.

Amazement filled his being;
The owl had not been wrong:
You cannot bring yourself to sing
Till you know where you belong.

June 1991

The Sanctuary

There upon the sheltered rock,
Above the babbling brook,
She sits alone—but never lonely—
And comprehends a second look.

Above her, bends a single tree
Whose branches drape the rock,
Providing her a natural tent—
Her hiding place, this spot.

And all around her, mountains,
Such solitude and strength;
They grant her thus a stillness,
Enabling her to think.

No one journeys out this way,
'Tis hers and hers alone.
A sanctuary of escape,
Yet not so far from home.

Cleansed by all about her,
A lightness fills her head.
Anxieties are minimized,
And daily boredoms shed.

Her thoughts ascend like puffs of clouds;
She grabs again at youth,
And while pretending age is lost,
She ignores the bitter truth.

Her fantasies are playful,
Lighthearted once again.
How glorious to sample
The way it was back then:

A simple spirit running free,
Romping here and there.
All of life ahead of her,
With dreams enough to share.

No need to fantasize the past;
'Twas still the early dawn,
With time enough to waste away,
Time to dance to every song.

The joy of contemplating love,
Of what the future holds;
Yet unforgetting of the ones
Who briefly held your soul.

The quickness of a youthful smile
That lights upon her face,
Content to stay and linger there
And not retreat in haste.

More years ahead than left behind,
With dreams to dwell upon,
Unafraid of passing days
Or time too quickly gone.

But that was very long ago,
Too long to know again.
So here upon my favorite rock,
I come to just pretend.

~

February 1995

Escape into Solitude

Where comes this need to be alone?
Many want to know.
Not even she can understand—
'Cept when it's time to go.

She packs her bag and bids goodbye
To those she truly loves.
They smile, but cannot really grasp
Why they are not enough.

Excitement fills her being,
While guilt invades her mind,
Why this need for solitude,
To leave them all behind?

A special place she runs to,
Quiet and serene.
Everything in order,
Like she strives for things to be.

No one calling out her name;
She issues no commands.
Everything is in its place,
Nothing out of hand.

Someone once suggested
Perfection's what she seeks.
And out here, where she runs to,
She finds its company.

Perhaps within his wisdom
He hit upon the truth:
A part of her is nurtured
By this perfect solitude.

And so I ask forgiveness
For this part of me I am,
And also seek acceptance
From those who cannot understand.

~

January 1997

Interlude of Mourning

Blindly racing up the road,
Tears tumbling down her face—
Her pounding heart, an aching load,
She hurried up her pace.

Very loved from where she came,
So why this quick escape?
She loves them, too, but still the same,
Her mind forbade her wait.

From the drudgery of dailiness,
She seeks a distant place
And once alone, to second-guess:
What made her leave in haste?

Is unfulfillment yet the cause
Or private, deep regrets—
A discontent with who she was,
Her life too firmly set?

But there she finds, like times before,
The faults remain her own.
'Twill always be her private war
To deal with self, alone.

Distance really matters not;
Miles won't change her woes.
The peace she ran away and sought
Hides deep within her soul.

Thus deciding, so she turns
To go from whence she came.
The pain she felt will cease to burn—
Till doubt creeps back again.

May 1991

Secrets In The Heart

A woman has many secrets,
And some she never shares.
Instead, she softly ponders
Those only her heart's aware.
A woman has many secrets,
A few comprised of guilt—
She tries to deeply hide them
But her heart won't let them wilt.
A woman has many secrets
She safely tucks apart
From all the rest of all the world
Except, of course, her heart.

~

September 1998

Secrets of the Past

Although the years appear, then fade,
The past remains behind.
But if that past holds secrets,
'Tis you, someday, they'll find.

No wrong can quite be buried
So deep it can't be found.
For every wrong there is a right
That says the wrong cannot stay down.

You don't know how or maybe when—
It may surface aft' you're gone.
Then what you thought you buried
Becomes alive and strong.

Beware today, the present, now'
Forego the wrongs along the way.
Alas, your past becomes the future—
And when it does, it comes to stay!

~

January 1999

The Used to Be's

The used-to-be's have disappeared;
The used-to-be's have gone.
So quietly, they slipped away;
They didn't last that long …

Something made them turn and leave,
Thus driving them away.
I may have seen the warnings
But knew not how to make them stay.

I think that *time* did play a part—
It changed the used-to-be's.
I saw them change, and then they left,
And only certain eyes could see.

I long to go and beg them back,
But doubt forbids I try—
Perhaps what's lost cannot be found
Once used-to-be's have died.

How sad I am without them;
I miss my used-to-be's.
And sadder still is knowing
What drove them 'way was … me.

~

September 1997

Sorrow in the Stillness

There's sadness here so late at night—
The darkness and the stillness shattered,
For speeding down yon country lane,
They race to that which matters.

Flashing lights and screaming sirens—
Their battle is to conquer time,
And once arrived to save a life,
I humbly watch; it isn't mine.

Safely sheltered upon my hill,
Warm and snug within my house,
In prayerful silence, I sit and watch
This fateful hour of someone else.

In little time, the rescue leaves;
The dark of night returns.
The country lane has fallen silent,
No trace of tragedy discerned.

One almost feels a twinge of guilt
To be so safe while others hurt.
Predictably, this hour passes,
But someone else's pain still lurks.

~

February 1995

The Fallen Innocent

The innocent are targeted.
The innocent lay dead,
As all across our nation
These violent acts have spread.

Buildings, schools, and stores—
Places not well known,
For now this Land of Freedom
Is killing yet its own.

Haven't all our many wars
Caused grief enough to bear?
So why these senseless shootings
That cause us more despair?

A city here, a hometown there,
A normal, routine day.
Then someone loses all control
And blows our peace away.

The tragedy draws headlines,
Consuming local news,
But once the crisis passes,
It fades but for a few.

These few, you see, are victims—
Their lives forever changed.
They and all their loved ones
Remain forever maimed.

You and I were lucky;
We escaped another's wrath—
But maybe next time, we'll be caught
Within his deadly path.

~

August 1999

Traitor in Our Midst

Another move, another home,
With guilty feelings all my own.
'Twas my undoing that got this done,
And now I'm feeling fairly stunned.
I'm well aware the pros and cons,
Reciting all the rights from wrongs.
But still these changes that I started
Have left a few so brokenhearted.
The past is like the roots of trees,
Buried deep and safe from thieves,
Until a selfish soul like me
Ruins all tranquility.
But still, I'm hoping—dare I hope?—
That, like the ship that steady floats,
There'll come a time when they will say
Their roots, again, feel safe today.
Long ago, my child once said:
Perhaps it's God within our heads
Who plants the seeds of certain thoughts
That first He planted in our hearts.
So maybe I'm not all to blame;
Perhaps another seed was laid.
But that is comfort just to me—
To all the world, a fool they see.

~

March 1999

The Fisherman

The Fisherman

Today I saw him fishing
From an isolated ramp.
He didn't know I saw him—
I was really glad for that.

He was sitting in a chair,
A chair with special wheels.
But still he sat there fishing,
Just himself, his rod, and reel.

It was certainly secluded,
A ramp for only one.
His back was to the passersby
While he faced the lowering sun.

I wondered, was he lonely
As he sat there so alone?
Or maybe while he's fishing,
He forgets the grief he's known.

A tragic deed has struck him
That forbids he'll ever stand—
But he won't deny the hobby
That made him a fisherman.

I admire so his courage—
He rose above his fate.
He chose to use the worms
And not himself as bait.

I bet he goes there often—
His spot upon the lake.
And maybe others dare to stop
To hear his story until late.

I found myself among them;
I could stop and be a friend.
But a nagging thought possessed me
As I drove past and round the bend.

What if he should ask me?
Would I have stopped and cared a lot
If I'd seen him *standing* on the ramp?
And I knew: no, probably not.

So I pray he wasn't lonely,
This fisherman alone.
But I'm not the one courageous
To invade this space he owns.

~

June 2000

Cycles

It never ceases to amaze me
What goes around comes back—
Like a haunting, vicious cycle,
It seeks you out and then attacks.

If you've ever said, *you'll never,*
You can bet someday you will.
And although you may deny it,
You know you're caught up hill!

A child will *never* be his parents,
Until that day he's grown
And finds himself repeating
Those patterns to his own.

An unkind turn to someone else,
Ignoring those in need—
Will someday work itself around
Till *you're* refused a kindly deed.

So often those we criticize
Do hurt the ones intended,
And then when we are criticized,
We are ever so offended.

A thing once mocked or hated
And put upon a shelf
Might someday so surprise us
To see it happening to ourselves.

But it seems it's human nature
To vow we'll never do
What we see so many doing—
Till the time it grabs us, too!

~

May 2000

Second Chance

No one seems to understand
No one seems to know—
Your friends, not knowing what to do—
They smile, then turn and go.

They talk of makeup, hair, and clothes,
What boy they long to date.
You think they all have passed you by,
But it's you with different traits.

A brush so close to death itself
Has left you hypnotized
With humbled thoughts and feelings
Of how you fought and thus survived.

You frolicked then as they do now
And told the same small lies.
But death did knock upon your door,
And now you see with opened eyes.

Trivial things of years ago
Are less important now.
Your view of life spans longer
Than once you dared allow.

But still you feel so ostracized:
Your friends have never danced
To such a song as you have—
Nor have they had a second chance.

So this you have to keep in mind:
How special that you are,
For surely God has chosen you
To be His shining star!

~

April 2000—for Kristen

Mirror, Mirror

Once upon a time ago
A woman held her looking glass
And hoped that she was pretty
But was far too shy to ask.

She was young and very able
For youth was on her side.
Her endless bouts of energy
Were a source of certain pride.

Unafraid to take a risk
A challenge spurred her on.
If she made a bad decision
She could say that she was wrong.

She loved the fun of something new
The quest to always try
To be the best that she could be
But knew that youth would hurry by.

And then Prince Charming came along
And swept her off her feet.
Again, her mirror told her
Surely pretty, surely sweet.

As years went by, and children came
Her youth did slip away.
Despite the work of little ones
She felt young enough to play.

Time marched on; the children grew
But the mirror stayed in place.
She could see her Prince was aging
And saw it too upon her face.

Still the years kept creeping by
Her offspring grown and gone.
But now that hanging mirror
Said indeed, there's something wrong.

Her face, her hair, her body
No longer looked the same.
And to the glass, she argued:
I don't feel this old and plain.

She well recalled the taste of youth
As though 'twas yesterday.
She told the glass it must be wrong:
My years could not have gone this way.

Take a look at what you see …
The mirror urged her on:
The graying hair, the wider waist
You're tired and not as strong.

But then her image in the mirror
Smiled despite itself—
Remembering what the mirror praised:
You've done well with what was dealt.

~

January 2002

Loose Ends

She sat in the inn, alone, by herself
Not knowing just quite what to do.
She questioned the act in coming at all,
Aware that her reasons were few.

Too late to go back, she looked at the walls—
Even the TV wasn't on.
She tried to read but tired too soon,
So lay on the bed till daylight was gone.

At first, it was peaceful, quiet as well;
Perhaps it was good that she came.
But when she awoke, the strangeness was there
And again, she felt just the same.

She called the one who could make it all right,
And as always, he knew what to say.
She hung up the phone with the confidence that
Tonight, where she was, she could stay.

~

February 2003

Fire

My neighbor's house burned down today;
Only the chimney stands.
How do you count for a loss like that?
Indeed, you never can.
A day ago, stood walls and rooms
And cozy, little nooks.
Gone are cherished treasures—
Pictures, albums, books.
A house will be constructed,
But years before it's home—
The walls will make it sturdy;
But 'twas the keepsakes that they owned
That surrounded them with pleasures
And gave comfort at day's end.
Now, nothing old or familiar
Can represent those "years of when."
The neighbors rally round to help,
And gifts of cash are made.
But none of us can ever know
The grief that in those ashes lay.
Tonight I go to bed and pray,
Glad and grateful it isn't me.
My neighbor's house burned down today;
The home they knew will never be.

~

June 2000

Nevermore

The farm is gone; the house is gone,
And also half our souls.
Gone the place we visioned
We would be when we were old.

Forces came together,
Unplanned and unforeseen.
And far too many choices
Wrecked a dream that might have been.

Too late to undo anything,
To cause it not to be.
And yet a tortured question
Is about to ruin me …

If indeed, we could go back
And keep things as they were—
Would we stay or journey on?
The pain is huge to be unsure.

Of this I know for certain,
Two souls I must have had,
'Cause now this hurting, empty hole
Has made one soul forever sad.

Someone else will know its walls
And walk upon its floors.
And every room's uniqueness
Will be a memory stored.

Nevermore the chance to feel
The warmth within its halls.
Nevermore to say it's ours—
Nevermore at all.

Why then the years of planning,
Such pain to make it true?
And then to only stay awhile—
From forever to a few?

Who caused this all to happen?
Who changed their minds amid
A dream so long awaited?
You did. I did. We did.

~

May 2, 2003

Feelings

Disappointed, disillusioned, dismayed
Hurting, hating, helpless
Ignored, indignant, indifferent
Lamenting, listless, lazy
Mad, madder, maddest
Needful, necessary, neglected
Private, personal, protected
Restless, resentful, remorseful
Sad, sadder, saddest
Taut, teased, terrible
Used, used, used
Void, void, void
Wishing, wanting, waiting
      Me

~

December 2001

Invisible Me

Don't look at me, don't look at me,
Don't look at me and see—
For you'll be disappointed
When you see who's really me.

Don't look at me, don't look at me,
Just look at someone else—
For it will make me happier
If you don't see myself.

Don't look at me, don't look at me,
Turn your head away.
Fix your gaze on yet another,
And maybe I will stay.

I'm here, but try to see me not,
Don't concentrate on me.
I appreciate your efforts
But it's best to let me be.

~

April 2000

The Mystery

They stop and stare and ponder,
They wonder what it means.
They stay a minute longer,
'Tis stranger than they've seen.
They leave, but still they're puzzled,
And while they walk away
They turn to take a second glance
At what they saw today.
Why would someone do that?
Their question stirs the air—
But they never know the answer,
For no one else is there.
There wasn't any written name,
Just a couple, simple lines:
Within here lies a mystery
That even she could not define.
The one who lies beneath this grave
Was well aware her name,
So she chose to leave it vacant—
'Tis she that you should blame.
For she was who decided
This phrase that once she planned ...
In life she so confused herself
Perhaps in death she understands.

~

April 2000

The Hermit

How will you know how to find me?
How will you know where to look?
Out of the midst, out of the way,
Hiding in a cranny or nook.

I'll be the one in the corner,
Not speaking, with little to say.
I'll be the one not mingling
In the spot I chose to stay.

I am the one who is waiting
For others to carry the show.
I am the one who is waiting
Till someone says I can go.

It is I who feels uneasy
Even among family and friends,
And this is what I ponder
While waiting for things to end.

How will you know how to find me?
How will you know where to look?
Seek out all the cubbyholes—
I'm hiding in a cozy nook!

~

August 2000

Solitary Road

Driving down the interstate
And through a busy town,
Buildings rose above me
On top of concrete ground.
Further down another road
Without the city lights,
Without the whirling traffic,
I could concentrate on life.
I passed a country graveyard
Where the grieved had come and "went."
So I said a silent prayer
For the one beneath the tent.
A humble, country farmhouse
Sat shaded by its trees,
While the weary farmer rested
And enjoyed a passing breeze.
There were horses in a pasture,
Children romping through a field.
I thought what simple pleasures
A quiet life could yield.
Then the dusk of day began,
When lights turn amber gold.
Even then, I wasn't lonely
Down that solitary road.

~

September 2005

On My Porch

I'm sitting on my porch,
Not very much to do,
And while I'm sitting here,
My thoughts go back to you.

They give me cause to smile,
And thus to reminisce,
To think of days gone by
And special times I miss.

With some, I've seen you recently,
With others, quite a while.
Some of you live fairly close,
But others, many miles.

For some, my thoughts are yesterday,
For others, years ago,
And saddened by the loss of time
We didn't get to know.

But I'm forever grateful
For those I've loved so much,
For all the different ways
Each "thought" my life has touched.

~

April 2010

Spur of the Moment

Things are bound to happen
When you least expect them to,
And surprisingly enough,
They mean the most to you.

A picture taken at the beach
Of your toddlers on the shore—
One you hadn't planned on
But will cherish ever more.

An outing never scheduled;
It didn't make your list,
But one you're ever thankful
Was not the one you missed.

The urge to give a compliment
You go ahead and say;
You answer yes to someone
So they'll have a better day.

Your husband throws a kiss good-bye
And heads to leave the door—
Suddenly you're running
To hug his neck once more.

Someone asks you how you are,
You start to say "not great";
Then you turn in time to see
His leg is in a brace.

Late one cold and winter night,
You wake your daughter up from sleep
To take a snowy midnight walk—
A memory you both will keep.

None of these were planned,
Yet done without delay—
Who could ever guess
The importance each would play?

~

October 2008

Fences in Our Lives

We've got many fences in our lives,
And some of them are great.
Especially those whose longest lengths
Stretch across our glorious state.

We've got rolling, cattle hillsides
With surrounding wooden fences,
To keep the cattle well inside
And the farmers sane, not senseless.

There are charming, country farmhouses
With pretty picket fences,
That keep its people well and strong—
Here, the fencing does the mending.

And many fences keep a dog
From wandering too far gone,
But yet allow him free to play
Within his yard all day long.

But there are fences in the body,
And equally as strong.
They stop their owners every day,
Saying *Halt, you can't go on.*

And what of fences of the mind,
That control our right-from-wrong?
How sad for some, these fences—
That cause their strength to crumble down.

But other, *mindful* fences
Are glad to see their strength
Play a part in how the day
Indeed was really meant.

So many different fences,
Some outward, some within—
And each one so important—
They make our days begin!

~

June 2010

VI

Ending Lantern

Dawn

Renewal

Though the day is gone
Still tomorrow lies in wait
Promising the dawn.

~